VICTORIAN YEARS

VICTORIAN YEARS

by
RAYMOND HARGREAVES

Ross Anderson Publications

Published in 1985 by
Ross Anderson Publications Limited
Larkhill House
160 St. Georges Road
Bolton BL1 2PJ

© Raymond Hargreaves 1985

All rights reserved. No part of this publication may be reproduced in any form or by any means, electronic or mechanical, including photo-copy, recordings, or any information, storage and retrievable system, without permission in writing from the publisher.

British Library Cataloguing in Publication Data

Hargreaves, Raymond
    Victorian Years
    1 Bolton (Greater Manchester) – Social Life and Customs
    I. Title
    942.7'37081   DA690.B65

ISBN 0 86360 024-7

Photoset in Linotron Plantin by
Northern Phototypesetting Co., Bolton
and printed in Great Britain by
Billings of Worcester

ACKNOWLEDGMENTS

I am, as always, grateful to the staff of the Bolton Reference Library for their willing help in providing the opportunity to study the volumes of the "Bolton Chronicle", and for their permission to reproduce the engravings contained in the "Bolton Almanack", which add so much to the 'flavour' of this story.

LOSTOCK, 1984   R. Hargreaves

COVER ILLUSTRATION BY ANNE HARGREAVES AND DESIGN BY ALAN PARKINSON

CONTENTS

Victorian Years – 1850 to 1860	1
Bolton – As It Was	3
The Poor	19
Crime and Punishment	39
The Industrious Poor	47
Holidays and Entertainment	61
Leisure and Pleasure	83
Religion	90
Politics	96
Medicine	105
War	117
Odd Items	135

ILLUSTRATIONS

Churchgate in 1846 (from Bolton Central Library by kind permission of the Bolton Metropolitan Borough Council)	7
The new Bolton Union Workhouse (*Bolton Almanac*)	37
Bolton's new Public Library (*Bolton Almanac*)	87
The Parish Church (*Bolton Almanac*)	93
One of Holloway's remedies (*Bolton Almanac*)	108
Another Holloway's remedy (*Bolton Almanac*)	109
The Infirmary and Dispensary (*Bolton Almanac*)	115
The new Market Hall (*Bolton Almanac*)	139
The 'deceitful and graceless' Crinoline (drawn by Anne Hargreaves)	141

FOREWORD

This is the story of the people of Bolton, and their environment in the Victorian Years of 1850 to 1860, as seen through the columns of the "Bolton Chronicle". Every aspect of daily life was reported in full, and the language and style evoke the atmosphere of the period. Bolton was a disreputable product of the Industrial Revolution, and in particular the upsurge of the cotton industry, which had been taken out of the cottage, and transferred to the myriad number of mills which could accommodate the new technology. Whilst this is the story of Bolton, other Lancashire towns had the same problems, the same attitudes, the same contrasts of wealth and poverty, and the same cycle of prosperity and depression. Engels in his report on "The Conditions of the Working Class in England 1844", remarked on Lancashire industrial towns that they were "mostly working class districts, interspersed only with factories, a few thoroughfares lined with shops, and a few lanes along which the houses and gardens of the manufacturers are scattered like villas. The towns themselves are badly and irregularly built, with foul courts and back alleys. Cellar dwellings are general here." Of Bolton in particular he observed it "has but one main street, a very dirty one, Deansgate, which serves as a market, and is even in the finest weather a dark unattractive hole." All, however, was not deep gloom, and progress, if slow, was made in many of the darker aspects of life in Bolton.

A new Workhouse was finally built; the Bolton Industrial Ragged School was opened to deal more humanely with juvenile delinquents and destitutes; more effort was being made to close many of the foul cellar dwellings; a new Public Library was provided, and a new Market Hall gave the opportunity to shop in more cordial surroundings.

The Crimean War and the Indian Mutiny attracted the same

patriotic fervour in Bolton as they did in other provincial towns, and the Editor of the Bolton Chronicle waxed eloquent on cause, event and solution in his Editorials. The American Civil War, which was to have a devastating effect on Lancashire cotton towns, did not break out and become a matter for concern until 1861, and there was still great expectation of continuing prosperity and progress in the coming years.

VICTORIAN YEARS
1850 to 1860

"Victoria's Heyday" is J. B. Priestley's descriptive title for the decade 1850 to 1860, and it is certainly apt when applied to the industrial wealth of the country, the freedom from any resource-bleeding European war, the might of her colonial empire, and the virtual monopoly of foreign trade in coal and iron, ships and steam engines, cotton and woollen textiles.

Bolton was sharing in the advantages and disadvantages of the great industrial surge; its middle-class prospered and had risen in authority and influence. There was no aristocratic over-lord, no influential landed gentry – the big landowners lived in other parts – so the mill owner, the merchant, the lawyer, the parson, filled the Council and the magistrates bench and sat on the Board of Guardians, and out of their number were M.P.'s elected.

As in the country as a whole, they were a mixture of some who were hypocritical, bigoted and small-minded, and some who were compassionate and eager for reform.

Much of the Cromwellian puritan conscience remained, but was mixed and interwoven with a materialistic morality. Prosperity had been founded on hard work and long hours, and this quality of hard work was now regarded as a paramount virtue, which was preached and advocated by Church and layman, and extolled as the road to salvation, both temporal and spiritual, for the poor.

Equally important was the precept of the liberty of the individual, a precept that was hurled at every attempt of reform. The individual had a right to keep a pile of dung in the street until he could get a good price for it; had a right to leave his machinery unfenced, the onus being on the worker not to get caught in it; had a right to rent his foul and miserable cellar to as many people as he could crowd into it.

The Established Church had, in the main, become the

preserve of the middle-classes, and the more prosperous of the working classes, attendance at Church being a required part of that aura of respectability which was a matter of great pride and importance to them. There was a great belief in and insistence on the acceptance of the station in life in which it had pleased God to have placed you. The now often deleted lines of a well known hymn –

> "The rich man in his castle, the poor man at his gate,
> God made them high or lowly and ordered their estate."

were sung with fervour and conviction.

Some of the benefits of prosperity were beginning to reach a few sections of the working classes. Textile operatives in the cotton trade had benefited from the passing and enforcement of the Factory Act. Boroughs were being encouraged to improve their environment, to get rid of the cellar dwellings, to take positive action to improve sanitation. Commissions were being set up by successive Governments, to report on practically every aspect of life affecting the masses of the underprivileged, but legislation was slow, and bitterly opposed at every stage.

Accommodation had never kept pace with the population explosion in the industrial towns like Bolton. The poor could not afford a whole house even in the poorest districts. Consequently overcrowding was rife from attic to cellar in buildings with little or no sanitary arrangements – no water taps and few privies.

It is not surprising that in their few hours of freedom the majority of the lower working classes sought relief from their cramped and miserable 'home', and took refuge in the warmth and bright lights of the concert room and pub, and solace in a pennyworth of beer or gin.

Crime and drunkenness were rife. Public executions, transportation, flogging, houses of correction, proved no deterrent. Temperance was preached as a solution in itself without advocating the removal of the root causes of intemperance.

In turning the pages of the weekly "Bolton Chronicle" for those years between 1850 and 1860, the reports, the editorials, the advertisements, the letters, all mirror a picture of the life and times in Bolton during "Victoria's Heyday".

BOLTON – AS IT WAS

There could be no better opening narrative than the Editorial which appeared in the Bolton Chronicle on 28th October 1854.

"An unsophisticated stranger to our town on taking up a copy of its local journal would be not unlikely to become the victim of a very pleasing delusion. If previously he had thought of Bolton as a thriving, and not unimportant manufacturing town only, a glance over the weekly "Chronicle" of its events might easily lead him to believe that he had unwittingly done it great injustice. . . . that Bolton was a paradise viewed morally, socially and intellectually; that it stood upon the very pinnacle of civilisation; that it was the place of all others where the best and purest and most gifted of mankind were congregated.

Unhappily, Bolton if no worse is certainly no better than the general run of manufacturing towns, and notwithstanding all its seeming activity in works of religious, moral, and intellectual improvement, there is, we regret to say, within its boundaries a vast floating population living without the fear, if not without the knowledge, of God in the world, intemperate and immoral, and who if they have acquired the arts of reading and writing, are certainly without the better part of education which consists in the development of moral nature. . . .

We are not speaking of the portion of the population usually characterised as the criminal class. We are speaking of men whose offences rarely expose them to the lashes of the law, we speak of men whose boast it is that they are of the producing class, that are of the "bone and sinew" of this land, and we say in all sorrow, but in all truth, that there are amongst even these no inconsiderable proportion who are as profligate, as improvident and as little removed from the brutes that perish as it is well possible for human beings to be.

Would this were libel; but unhappily the experience of every man intimately acquainted with the condition of the working classes in our own town attests the truth of the statement. It attests this other truth also, that there is no foundation in justice for the answer so often made . . . because they are ground down by the 'cotton lords', who while rolling in riches themselves pay their workmen scarcely sufficient to 'keep body and soul together.'

Now we are not about to enter into the defence of the 'tyrant cotton lords', the time may come indeed in which we shall have something to say about their short comings with respect to the thousands they employ.

Here, until the last few months, our staple manufactures have been in great demand, our mills and foundries consequently in active operation and the workers in full and constant employment. For a long time there were hundreds, if not thousands, of men who earned weekly very high wages, 30s, 40s and in some cases 50s a week was not an uncommon sum. What was the consequence? Were the men so long "ground down" found anxious and ready to seize their golden opportunity to better their fortunes. Did they remove to better dwellings or cleanse and refurnish the old? Did they put a little away for the inevitable "rainy day" or exempt their wives and children from toiling in the factory, that the former might increase the comfort of the home, and the latter have those educational advantages necessarily denied them in "hard times"?

Alas, none of these things did they do, of exceptions there have been many and thankful we are of them, but as a rule those who had been "unsteady" before became absolute drunkards now; their homes remained filthy and wretched as ever. Neither schools, nor churches, nor savings banks bore pleasing testimony to their thrift and increased means. The one striking result was that men who dared not so absent themselves when work was scarce, thought nothing now of allowing their places to remain vacant for half a week after each pay day. . . .

18/11/54

. . . and we next, therefore, address a word or two to the employers of labour. Do they really make the attempt to lead industry in the right path? Do they really trouble themselves about the happiness of those in their employ? Do they take anything like an active and sympathetic interest in the domestic and the personal condition of their labourers? Do they distinguish by their countenance, and favour those whose habits are temperate and self-denying? As a rule we fear not. We fear the majority of employers concern themselves only to see that their operatives do their allotted work and for aught besides – whether the men squander their earnings in a beer shop or carry them home for the use of their family, whether they live in filthy cellars or in comfortable cottages, whether they send their children to school or allow them to grow up neglected vagabonds, whether they go to the Free Library and the Mechanics Institute, or to the Socialist meeting and the Chartist assembly – in short, whether they are a blessing or a pest to society at large – it never once enters their minds to ascertain. This is a grave neglect for which the amplest donations to religious and educational institutions will never compensate."

This contemporary article depicts Bolton inhabited by irresponsible people, the working class neglectful of themselves, the middle class neglectful of their employees. It is doubtful whether the truth was quite so clearly defined. No skill or prudence could protect a man from prolonged sickness and resultant poverty. The best of wages left little enough margin to save, and in the textile trades there were spasms of depression that came with regular frequency and were accepted as the normal trade cycle.

In cotton towns like Bolton the depressions affected the majority of people, for here Cotton was King. Many employers were equally affected for they were not all men of substance, some were only a little better off than those they employed, and prolonged depressions resulted in bankruptcy.

What sort of environment did these people of Victorian Bolton live in?

A picture emerges of cobbled streets and horse dung, hovels and tenements, town houses and concert halls, factories and forges, filth and smells, soot laden atmosphere, and very little of an attractive nature. Some of the seamier side is reflected in the Borough Police Report:

BOLTON CHRONICLE 2nd November 1850
"*BOROUGH POLICE STATISTICS*
There are in the Borough 117 inns and public houses, 163 beerhouses for selling on the premises and 9 beerhouses for selling off the premises. Total 289.
Public houses and beerhouses having musical entertainments 14; having dancing as well as music 11; where thieves resort 15; where gambling is practised 15; houses at which it is supposed spirituous or fermented liquors are sold without licence 31.
Pawnbrokers 20; Dealers in lead, brass, rags, etc., 59; Dealers in gold and silver plate, jewellery etc., 28.
Brothels in the Borough 37, six having been suppressed during the year.
The prostitutes are stated to be 78.
Reputed thieves in the Borough 71, or three less than last year.
Number of streets in the Borough 474.
Dwelling houses 10,799, of which 486 were unoccupied.
Cellars used as dwellings 1,715 of which 136 were unoccupied.
Places of Public Worship 28."

The brothels outnumbered the churches, and the impressive number of pubs and beerhouses provided the Temperance advocates with a formidable task of reform, and the number of brothels supported their claim of moral decadence associated with intemperate habits. John Green, a native of Lostock, writing in 1846 from Handsworth to friends in Chew Moor, was evidently struck by the absence of prostitutes in his new location, for he writes

> "I have never seen a bedgown except one since I left, and that was in Birmingham . . . who I supposed to be a Liverpool or Manchester merchant, for it was dark and she was followed by numerous customers."

"Bedgown" is a somewhat quaint term for the ladies of easy virtue, and seems to imply that they were 'dressed' (or should that be undressed) ready for work!

Whilst dealing with statistics the census of 1851 gives the composition of the Bolton Union and compares the populations of 1841 and 1851.

BOLTON CHRONICLE 3rd May 1851

	Population 1851	1841
Greater Bolton	39,923	33,609
Little Bolton	20,469	16,144
Bradshaw	853	827
Breightmet	1,540	1,309
Edgeworth	1,230	1,697
Entwistle	486	555
Farnworth	6,374	4,829
Halliwell	3,959	3,242
Harwood	2,056	1,996
Heaton	826	713
Horwich	3,942	3,774
Little Hulton	3,184	3,052
Middle Hulton	888	902
Over Hulton	452	445
Kearsley	4,235	3,435
Darcy Lever	2,090	1,701
Great Lever	713	657
Little Lever	3,512	2,580
Longworth	152	149
Lostock	620	625
Quarlton	361	370

Churchgate in 1846 (from Bolton Central Library by kind permission of the Bolton Metropolitan Borough Council)

	Population	
	1851	*1841*
Rumworth	1,386	1,298
Sharples	3,904	2,879
Tonge with Haulgh	2,826	2,627
Turton	4,158	3,577
Westhoughton	4,549	4,527

The end of cottage industry, and the gradual absorption of the smaller farms into larger units, resulted in the decline of population in the country districts, as people drifted into the towns to find employment. Out of the 380 houses in Edgeworth 123 were unoccupied. The total population of the Union had risen from 97,519 in 1841 to 114,688 in 1851.

Following the Municipal Corporations Act of 1836, Bolton was one of the first towns to apply for incorporation. The application provoked a long and bitter controversy, and there were petitions and deputations to the Government of the day, followed by counter-petitions and counter-deputations. The opponents of the idea of Incorporation continued the fight after the Queen had granted a Charter of Incorporation on 11th October 1838, and a Town Council had been elected. There was further agitation and litigation which was only terminated by an Act of Parliament passed in 1842, which established the validity of the Charter of Incorporation previously granted. The Great and Little Bolton Trustees, who had been the Town authority until Incorporation, still exercised rights with regard to paving and lighting the streets, but the passing of the Bolton Improvement Act, in 1850, saw their powers and property transferred to the Corporation. In addition to consolidating the powers and authority of the Corporation the Act incorporated the provisions of the Public Health Act, 1848, and the Towns Police Clauses Act of 1847. There were special provisions for the erection of a Market Hall, and for supplying water to various districts surrounding the Borough.

The sanitary condition of the town was a major concern of the Corporation, for the fear of Cholera was always present, though it took outbreaks in other parts of the country to hasten positive action.

BOLTON CHRONICLE 11th June 1853
"SANITARY CONDITION OF BOLTON

Too much attention to the sanitary condition of the Borough cannot be paid at any time, but more especially during the present hot weather, when atmospheric impurities and noxious effluvia arising from surcharged cesspools and putrid matter which has been allowed to accumulate upon our middensteads, tend to engender disease and to foster those epidemics which if not checked in time would soon decimate our population.

Attention to cleanliness and to proper ventilation are matters of deep concern to every inhabitant of the borough; and it is particularly gratifying to find that the members of our Sanitary Committee are now bestirring themselves with more than ordinary activity in the removal or suppression of nuisances and in providing for the general improvement of the town. These efforts cannot fail to be productive of the most beneficial results, and we trust that in their exertions to promote the health and welfare of the town the Committee will receive the cordial assistance of the inhabitants at large.

With a view to more stringent enforcement of the law and to secure the co-operation of the Magistrates in this respect a deputation from the Sanitary Committee waited on the Borough Magistrates.

Mr. Alderman Parkinson stated the views and object of the deputation.

Mr. Parkinson did not find fault with the decisions of the Bench but merely asked their assistance in the removal of nuisances. He adverted to the removal of night soil in which much difficulty had been experienced, farmers frequently refused to fetch it away as worthless. Mr. Parkinson called the particular attention of the Magistrates to the disgraceful state of the River Croal, which in consequence of the filth daily thrown into it was almost dammed up.

The Committee had for a long time been aware of the difficulty of cleaning the river Croal; and when they took into account that parties brought before the Bench had been merely fined 2s. 6d. for putting probably a hundred cart loads of cinders in the river, the difficulty became greater still. There were factories, foundries and bleachworks which emptied all their cinders in the Croal, there were also numerous parties which emptied all their filth into the river, and unless these cases could be more vigorously dealt with than heretofore it would be out of the power of the Sanitary Committee to do their duty. It was not the poor, but the rich who could afford to pay who put these cinders in the river, and therefore ought to be proceeded against.

The deputation then thanked the Bench for the courtesy with which they had been received and withdrew."

In September 1853 there was an outbreak of Cholera in various parts of the country. The Bolton Chronicle in an editorial lashed the Authorities for the filthy state of the town, and the ineffectual action taken to prevent the outbreak of an epidemic.

24th September 1853   Editorial
"The pestilence is once more amongst us! and how has the plague found us after such a lapse of time? Have we benefited by the dear-bought lessons of experience? How had we prepared ourselves for the present visitation? Rather should we ask, have we made any preparation whatsoever for this pestilence?

In one sense it may perhaps be said that we have prepared ourselves for its advent. We have invited its presence in all our populous towns and cities, by our culpable neglect of all sanitary precautions, by our utter disregard of cleanliness, by our negligence in the drainage of streets, lanes and alleys, and more than all, by permitting accumulations of all kinds of offensive and putredinous matter to go on undisturbed, we have actually made every preparation in our power to increase the virulence of the cholera, and to augment the number of its victims.

It is no use for us to plead that this dreadful scourge has come upon us unawares. We have had an opportunity for many months past of watching its silent progress through the east and north of Europe.

Let us now take a survey of the town and then pronounce upon the culpability or otherwise of the Town Council.

In whatever direction we move we shall not have to travel far before we meet with cesspools "running over" into the very streets, dungheaps reeking with all imaginable kinds of filth, drains and gutters streaming with all kinds of impurities, offensive trade operations carried on, from which the sickening smells continually arise, stagnant pools of water constantly emitting the most deleterious mephitic gases, houses devoid of those conveniences which decency as well as cleanliness renders indispensable, and, in short, the most palpable proofs of the presence in rank luxuriance of every description of abominable nuisance, calculated alone to engender disease, and certain, in case of the appearance of cholera amongst us, to aggravate its horrors and to increase its fatality.

For this state of things somebody must be to blame. In many instances private individuals are the culpable parties, wherever they have neglected the most obvious precautions against the accumulation of filth and ordure, wherever landlords have wilfully neglected to provide sufficient drainage for their property, or suitable accommodation to ensure some degree of cleanliness on the part of their tenants; they must be pronounced guilty of gross and unpardonable conduct, and public opinion will not fail to point them out, whatever their station in life. But the chief blame must rest on the shoulders of our Public Authorities. Invested as they are with ample powers to remove or abate nuisances of all descriptions, the fact that such nuisances are found to exist among us, is a proof of gross negligence and grave dereliction of duty.

Let not the cry of "vested interests" deter the authorities from the faithful and vigorous discharge of their duties. The public health is a matter of paramount consideration before which private rights ought to give way and must give way.

Let every man act during the present visitation as if the spread or prevention of the dire pestilence rested on his own individual exertions or example."

An official return issued on 1st October 1853 showed that in Eastern Bolton there were one case of Cholera, 6 cases of diarrhoea and two cases of Typhus fever, with seven cases of diarrhoea in Western Bolton, 1 case of diarrhoea and 1 case of dysentery in Little Bolton.

Advice issued by the General Board of Health was published in the Bolton Chronicle on 1st October 1853;

"*PLAIN ADVICE DURING THE VISITATION OF THE CHOLERA*
After the necessity of cleanliness in streets, dwellings and persons has been urgently enforced, the following recommendations are given:–

If an attack, even the slightest, should come on in your household you must immediately apply for medical assistance. Arrangements will be made in every locality to render such assistance promptly and effectually. There is no disease which can be more readily met than Cholera in its first or premonitory stage.

In cases of diarrhoea or looseness of the bowels, the following medicine is recommended by the Board of Health, but avoid if you can, exercising your own judgement in giving medicine at all: 20 grains of opiate confection mixed with two tablespoonfuls of peppermint water, or with a little weak brandy and water, and repeated every three or four hours, or oftener if the attack is severe. Half the quantities to persons under 15, smaller doses to children. If the disease assumes a violent form before help can be obtained, put the sufferer into a warm bed, apply bottles of hot water or heated flannel to the stomach and feet and along the spine. A dessertspoonful of brandy may be given from time to time in hot water. Constant friction with flannel dipped in hot vinegar is recommended, as well as the application of a vinegar and mustard poultice over the belly. A prudent person will have the necessary articles at hand, but promptitude in getting assistance is the first duty. By night or by day send for the doctor, and such is the zeal of the medical profession that the humblest person will not send in vain."

Twelve months later there was a further threat of a cholera epidemic, and further attempts were made to arouse the Corporation and the public to preventative action.

BOLTON CHRONICLE 5th August 1854

"Intimations frequent enough are furnished by the newspapers to convince us that the cholera still lingers amongst us in its most virulent epidemic type. Among the proximate causes of cholera may be reckoned the more local features of unwholesome habitations, crowded rooms, ill-ventilated courts and alleys, collections of decayed organic matter in the midst of densely peopled streets, accumulations of filth in cesspools, overflowing drains rank with abominable and noxious effluvia, intramural interments in old graveyards filled with corpses, to the very surface of the ground, putrefying dungheaps, and other sources of noxious miasmata.

It is scarcely necessary that we should repeat that all these causes are to be found in great abundance in Bolton, but it is needful that we should again and again urge their removal. Notwithstanding the alleged energy which has been brought to bear upon the removal of nuisances, they are still rife enough in every locality.

The stench which arises from the sewers is a nuisance which prevails in all directions. During the late dry weather the effluvium from the sewers was intolerably offensive."

9th September 1854

"Considerable activity has been manifested by the authorities in order, as far as possible, to preserve the health of the town. Yesterday the special Committee of Guardians and members of the Town Council inspected a considerable portion of the Borough, ordering the removal of many nuisances, etc.

The following suggestions as to the precautions to be observed have been printed at the expense of the Corporation for extensive circulation:-

1. Apply to a medical man immediately in case of looseness of the

bowels, as it may bring on cholera.
2. Do not take any salts or other strong medicine without proper advice.
3. Beware of drink; for excess in beer, wine or spirits is likely to be followed by cholera.
4. Avoid eating meat that is tainted or unwholesome, decayed or unripe fruit and stale fish and vegetables.
5. Avoid fasting too long. Be moderate at meals.
6. Avoid great fatigue or getting heated and then chilled.
7. Avoid getting wet or remaining in wet clothing.
8. Keep yourself clean, and your body and feet as dry and as warm as your means and occupation will permit.
9. Keep your rooms well cleaned and whitewashed. Open the windows as often as possible. Remove all dirt and impurities immediately.
10. Use chloride of lime or zinc to remove any offensive smells.
11. If there are any dust or dirt heaps, foul drains, bad smells or other nuisances in the house or neighbourhood, make a complaint without delay to the local authorities having legal power to remove them."

On the 9th September 1854, the Inspector of Nuisances was reporting three cases of cholera to the Town Council.

BOLTON CHRONICLE 9th September 1854
TOWN COUNCIL
"His Worship the Mayor then read the following report from the Inspector of Nuisances.
"To the Sanitary Committee.
Gentlemen,
I regret to say that three cases of cholera have occurred during the past week in this town, two of which terminated fatally, and the other has so far recovered as to be out of further danger.

The first case was that of Joseph Crosby residing in Mechanic Street, in a confined yard 13 feet by 15 feet long into which one other house opens, and two others abut, leaving only a three foot passage ingress and egress, without any through ventilation. The house in question presents dirty walls and ceiling, the floor partly covered with broken flags, the remaining portion being unflagged; no ventilation from windows, an offensive drain in the yard alluded to. Deceased was a cardroom hand, 33 years old, said to be of steady habits; was taken ill on Tuesday morning at 10 o'clock, and died on Wednesday morning at 2 o'clock. Was attended by Doctor Cawthorne who pronounced it a decided case of Asiatic Cholera.

The second case was a man about 40 years old, residing in a cellar at the top of Cross Street, said to have been of dissipated habits;

taken ill on Tuesday and died on Friday morning at six o'clock. The floor, walls and ceiling dirty; no ventilation. When I visited the place there were about half-a-dozen dirty children and four or five adults in the place, besides two small children in a cradle, one apparently in a dying state. This man was attended by Doctor Carruthers, who had no doubt of it being a clear case of Asiatic Cholera. The third case, of a man living in Sharples Court, Back Chapel Street, who was taken ill about the time of the first case, but was out of danger this afternoon. This Court is about 15 yards long by about 5 yards wide, having an entrance passage 3 feet wide in the centre, but no thoroughfare. There is a cesspool at the end of the yard adjoining the houses, the soakings from which tend to make the house damp, whilst the reeking exhalations rise to the chamber window. I am informed that there were thirteen cases of bowel complaint at one mill on Friday last, but the owner in each case supplied an immediate antidote, and no worse consequences followed. In conclusion I beg to state that, notwithstanding the above cases, the town is generally in a healthy condition, and no additional cases have occurred up to four o'clock this day.
I am, Gentlemen,
  Your obedient servant,
    R. Carling."

The Sanitary Committee ordered the Inspector to compel the owner or occupier to cleanse, whitewash and purify any dwelling house which in his opinion was in a filthy and unwholesome condition. The special Committee appointed by the Council in September last made almost a house to house visitation and ordered the removal of an immense number of nuisances, and he thought similar proceedings would be adopted with much advantage on the present occasion.

Mr. James Haslam inquired whether the proposed visitation was for sanitary purposes as well as for the prevention of cholera.

The Mayor said it had no connection with sanitary proceedings but merely as a preventative of disease. The only cases of cholera which had occurred in this town were in dirty and ill-ventilated places. With regard to sanitary matters Lord Palmerston had ordered that all graveyards in the Borough should be closed in March next. The vestry had power to provide cemeteries, but they had not hitherto exercised that authority. He understood the Council were not willing to take this question up, and left it in the hands of the Churchwardens; but steps must be taken to prevail upon the latter to do their duty.

Some conversation ensued, in which it was again stated that the whole responsibility of the matter rested with the Churchwardens who had received the precept; and if they wanted the assistance of the Council it was their duty to ask for it."

The Public Health Act of 1848 made provision for the closure of cellar dwellings which did not conform to a certain standard, but the enforcement of the Act raised problems; if you closed the cellar what did you do with the tenants? They couldn't afford the rent of better class accommodation even if it were available, and perhaps even more to be considered was the landlord who would lose his rent; after all it was the landlord who was on the roll of electors, not the tenant.

Bolton procrastinated, action being postponed for five years, and in 1855 took the first positive step towards closure.

BOLTON CHRONICLE 17th March 1855
"NOTICE
Borough of Bolton – Township of Great Bolton
NOTICE IS HEREBY GIVEN, that from and after the ninth day of August next, it will not be lawful to let or occupy, or suffer to be occupied, separately as a dwelling within the Borough of Bolton, any vault, cellar or underground room of a certain description defined by the 67th Section of the Public Health Act 1848, and that the owner and occupier of any such vault, cellar or underground room will each be liable to a penalty of 20s per day for every day the same be so occupied."

A week before the provisions of the notice became operative the Bolton Chronicle Editorial had comment to make.

4th August 1855
"CELLAR DWELLINGS
A return procured in 1848 gives the following as the 'cellar population' of some of the principal towns in Lancashire –
Bolton 4,961
It is horrible to think of the manner in which so many thousands of human beings are huddled together in these miserable cellar dwellings, breathing a foul and vitiated atmosphere during the greater portion of their existence, and hastening to their premature graves through seasons of protracted and often unbroken sickness.

By Clause 4 of the Bolton Improvement Act (1850) the time for closing these cellars was postponed for five years which time expires on Thursday next. It is computed that about 1,000 cellars in the town are not in compliance with the terms of the Act and will have to be eventually closed. We do not think it would be at all wise to enforce the Act at once in the case of the whole thousand. This would inflict a very great hardship upon hundreds of families who would thus suddenly be deprived of shelter, not to say anything about the injury which would be inflicted upon the owners of such property.

The evils attending the cellar system are too flagrant not to demand a remedy, but that remedy may be temperately and judiciously applied without a too vigorous application of the law."

Three years later the Editor was advocating a more rigorous attitude.

BOLTON CHRONICLE 13th November 1858
Editorial
"SANITARY CONDITION OF BOLTON
The river Croal is one gigantic and unbroken nuisance in warm and dry seasons, generating as it does on its torpid and sinuous course, through the most densely populated parts of the town, the foulest and most deadly miasmata. This monster grievance will have to be dealt with boldly, but with every legitimate regard to vested rights. Let it not, however, be forgotten that the most indefeasible of vested rights is that which a bountiful Providence has conferred upon every man, woman and child – the right of breathing an uncontaminated atmosphere.

With regard to the closing of cellar dwellings, the Sanitary Committee ought to come to an immediate decision. There can be no room for doubt or hesitation on this point. It is absolutely necessary that the use of a large number of them should be imperatively forbidden. It may be a question whether the owners are, or are not, entitled to compensation. In other boroughs an indiscriminate closing of cellars has taken place without any regard whatever being paid to such claims.

The general unhealthiness of cellar dwellings is now universally recognised. They are often found to be the nuclei whence the most pestilent fevers are found to radiate. The Sanitary Committee will do no more than its duty, under the provision of the Acts which are now in force in the Borough, by ordering all cellars to be shut in which there is not the requisite conformity with the terms of the law."

Later in the month the closure of cellar-dwellings was raised at a meeting of the Town Council.

BOLTON CHRONICLE 27th November 1858
"TOWN COUNCIL MEETING – CLOSING OF CELLAR DWELLINGS
In August 1855 when the Council first took proceedings to enforce

the closing of cellars as dwellings there were in the Borough 1,600 cellars occupied as dwellings by some 6,000 persons.

In 1856 128 cellars were closed as dwellings, in 1857 49, and in 1858 13.

Alderman Ferguson proposed 'That it be an instruction from this Council to the Sanitary Committee to continue the closing of cellar dwellings.'

Mr. Nicholson rose for the purpose of opposing the resolution, he did it because he thought it was unjust. It interfered with a class of property that was highly assessed and highly taxed. The Council were asked to close these cellars and thereby destroy one third portion of the income of the owners.

The habits of the people, their natural constitution, the food they ate and the liquor they drank, had in his opinion a great deal to do with their health, perhaps more than had cellar dwellings.

As to the working people who dwelt in cellars, many of them spent only a very small portion of their time in them. Take the case of a working man and his wife, for instance, they went to work between five and six in the morning and were away all day, except an hour and a half of meal times, until between six and seven in the evening. Therefore, they did not breathe the impure air that was described.

The motion was carried. Mr. Nicholson alone voted against, but several did not vote."

Although Mr. Nicholson's opposition received no support, his attitudes reflect the sentiments of a section of the middle and upper classes. This unfeeling attitude towards the poor was merely an extension of the belief that a just God had ordained their station in life, and they, the poor, should accept their lot uncomplainingly, and, besides pandering to their wants, any charity to relieve their position would merely encourage them to produce more children, and further increase the pauper population, to the great distress of the ratepayer.

At the end of 1860 there were still 1,068 occupied cellar dwellings. A number of these would no doubt meet the requirements of the Public Health Act, and a Mr. Taylor refers to these dwellings in his personal recollections –

"My Grandfather rented a shop in Newport Street, the second from Great Moor Street on the other side. The living room was in the cellar; all the shops and dwelling houses in Newport Street had cellars, most of them tenanted. In some cases the tenants occupied the cellars only, living and sleeping in them. They looked clean habitations, the steps to them so clean that one hesitated to go down. Callers usually shouted or knocked on the cellar window, which had a lace curtain, just above the curtain was a shelf for geraniums and a sweet smelling musk plant. . . . The yard or back area was about six feet wide, enclosed by a wall, shutting out the sunlight, and causing a stuffy, damp atmosphere. The yard and lavatory was common to the four shops, at some earlier period there was a well in the yard which supplied the tenants, and probably the neighbourhood. The well was four feet in diameter, lined with brick. This row of shops had the ground floor above the street level and had about four stone steps in the year 1868, about that time the floor was lowered to the street level; the cellars were excavated and some of the debris thrown into the well. Grandfather's cellar was unfit for habitation as a result, and for this reason my Grandfather decided to quit the premises."

THE POOR

Poverty was never on one level, there was class distinction among the poor; grades of misery. At the bottom were the destitute with not even the meanest cellar as an habitation. Numbered among these were the drunkards and drifters, the chronic sick, the limbless ex-soldiers and many aged. A little higher in the poverty stakes were those who depended on odd jobs to earn a copper, the orphans and unwanted children who scrounged and stole in order to exist, the temporary sick with no wages, and still a little higher the unskilled labourer. The ranks of all these grades were increased as periodical trade depressions hit the town, and thousands were out of employment. At least on these occasions the problem became so acute that notice had to be taken, and there was such an occasion in 1855.

BOLTON CHRONICLE 17th February 1855
"CONDITION OF THE POOR
Owing to the unusual severity of the season and to the general depression of trade, want and its concomitant evils have become exceedingly prevalent in several of our large manufacturing towns, and not the least so in our own Borough. The cessation of employment, or the curtailment of the hours of labour, or the inadequate renumeration for many descriptions of work, may be enumerated among the chief causes of the great mass of suffering to which the operative and other classes in this town have been for some time subjected. The distress thus arising from the want of employment is still further aggravated by the high price of food and severity of the weather. If a change in the condition of our poor is not speedily affected or if relief is not afforded to them, so as to give them a suitable supply of wholesome food, and to screen them from the inclemency of the weather, there is but too much reason to fear that the present distress will superinduce disease. We were going to close our remarks by urging upon the public of Bolton the necessity of some movement in favour of our suffering poor, but we are glad

to find that we have been anticipated in our appeal, and that the people of Bolton have already 'pronounced' in favour of their distressed neighbours."

"NOTICE
At a meeting of the inhabitants of Bolton held in the Borough Court on Friday, February 16th, to consider the best means of alleviating the distress now prevailing in the borough from the number of persons out of employment, his Worship the Mayor presiding, it was moved by the Rev. T. Berry, seconded by Robert Heywood, Esq., and carried unanimously:
'That this meeting deeply deploring the great distress now prevailing in the borough from the number of persons out of employ, considers that immediate measures should be adopted to alleviate the distress as much as practicable'."

As a result of this meeting a Distress Fund was established. Organised charity was the Victorians' inevitable answer to distress. Subscription lists were published weekly in the papers, and it was the right and proper thing to ensure your name appeared. No doubt publication encouraged reluctant givers, and such organised charity ensured that it was the 'deserving' poor who profited, and the 'undeserving' left to consider the error of their ways.

With such widespread and dire poverty the Poor Law Board of Guardians had to cope with a mass of applications for relief. A report was made at a meeting of the Guardians on 3rd March 1855.

BOLTON CHRONICLE 3rd March 1855
"BOARD OF GUARDIANS
The Relief Fund
The Relief Fund is doing its duty in a very effectual manner. Owing to the great number of applications there has been unavoidable delay in visiting many applicants, but the number of visitors has been increased and the inconveniences considerably remedied. The families relieved amount already of upwards of 2,000, and applications are still pouring in. We do hope that this statement will appeal powerfully and successfully to the Christian public for an increase of liberal support.

On Wednesday morning the old soup kitchen in Old Hall Street was opened and 500 quarts of excellent soup distributed among the poor people. Yesterday morning 1,200 quarts were served out, and this morning another 1,200 quarts were to be distributed. In addition to this vast numbers have been relieved with bread, meal and potatoes. Coal has also been distributed, 75 tons of good housecoal having been placed at the disposal of the Committee by W. H. Hulton, Esq., and 10 tons by Messrs. R. & T. Thompson, in addition to the 50 tons given by Messrs. Knowles & Sons last week."

Charity and mercy did certainly exist, time, energy and money were freely given by many Boltonians, and their efforts without doubt averted starvation and alleviated the misery of vast numbers of workless.

BOLTON CHRONICLE 5th May 1855
"THE DISTRESS FUND
A meeting of the Subscribers to this fund was held at the Poor Protection Society's Office, New Market Place, yesterday, to receive the general report of the Committee and to determine how the balance remaining should be disposed of.

The report showed that a vast amount of distress had been relieved since the appointment of the Committee.

The public subscription amounted to £1,086. 11s. 6d. and of this sum £951. 6s. 1d. had been expended leaving in hand at the present time a balance of £135. 5s. 5d. On the motion of Mr. Stockdale it was resolved that the operations of the Committee should continue in consequence of the hands still out of employ."

The gradual improvement of trade saw re-employment and a weekly wage going into the household. Even with re-employment there must have been a long term effect which would drag families down to miserable poverty levels. There were rent arrears to be paid off, clothes and furniture to be taken out of pawn, credit at the corner shop and pub to be repaid – and always living with the constant fear that sickness or unemployment would appear or recur before existing debts had been cleared, leading to the then final degradation of the workhouse and a pauper's grave.

THE POOR LAW AND THE BOARD OF GUARDIANS

The spectre of the 'workhouse' hovered constantly over the poor, and to the 'deserving' poor must have been a never ending and horrid nightmare.

The Poor Law of 1601 was completely inadequate to deal with problems of the 1800's, for its provisions catered for small parishes and static populations, the poor of which could be adequately supported by the local poor rate. These provisions, this system, could not possibly cope with the growth of towns and cities in the industrial explosion, and the migration of people from countryside to towns. It could not determine which parish was responsible for the drifting population, and no parish was wealthy enough to meet the demands of large scale unemployment.

Victorian economists like Thomas Malthus and Harriet Martineau had wide support for their views that the poor should be suppressed, that charity and relief should not be given, for this only encouraged the poor to produce more children, and so add even more to the pauper numbers. The poor should be discouraged even if it meant starving them.

In 1833 the Commissioners appointed to report on the Poor Law stated that outdoor relief acted as a "national provision for discouraging the honest and industrious and protected the lazy, vicious and improvident and encouraged early marriages and large families."

As a result of this report a new Poor Law became effective in 1834, which provided that parishes were to amalgamate into "Unions", and have control of workhouses to serve the whole "Union". Relief outside the workhouse was to be kept to the absolute minimum, relief inside the workhouse was to be repaid by work.

There was some intention that the sick, the aged, the very young – the deserving poor – should be reasonably cared for, and the idle, the wastrel, the drunkard – the undeserving poor – should be treated with harshness and intolerance.

Unfortunately the dividing line was never properly established, and all, deserving or undeserving, suffered equally.

The food supplied in the workhouse had to be in quantity and quality less than the miserable poor outside the walls were getting – otherwise all the poor would be clambering for admittance. If families were admitted then they must be ruthlessly segregated, wife from husband, children from parents. Co-habitation might result in even more children. Work was to be done in repayment for the food and shelter provided, but this too raised a problem. If proper productive work was done in the workhouse it would compete with outside businesses – so useless work had to be found; picking oakum or breaking stones.

Bolton Poor Law Union comprised 26 parishes and 32

'Guardians' were elected to the Board to represent the Ratepayer's interests, and to put into action the requirements of the Poor Law.

Bolton's elected guardians were fully representative of the middle class gentry, the land agent, the farmer and shopkeeper, the mill owner, the merchant, the parson, the lawyer, and epitomised Victorian morality and sentiment. They were probably no better or no worse than in other towns, but they do not emerge with any great commendation, for at times even the Poor Law Board Inspector was critical of the Guardians' treatment of and attitude towards the poor under their jurisdiction.

It is to the credit of the minority that they strived to ameliorate the condition of the 'deserving poor', and succeeded over the years in obtaining improvements in their treatment and conditions. The press too played its part in attempting to persuade the Guardians to adopt a more humane attitude to their charges. Many Guardians were intransigent and unmoved by the appalling conditions and plight of the poor, to 'save the ratepayer's money' was their only concern and duty, and the only mandate given to them on their election to office.

The Guardians decided and directed policy, the Overseers, also elected into office by the ratepayers, implemented the policies, and dealt directly with the supplicant poor, deciding whether a shilling outdoor relief would suffice, or whether the applicant was so destitute as to warrant a place inside the workhouse.

The Union workhouse was an inadequate set of buildings in Fletcher Street, and a further workhouse at Turton was maintained mainly to house destitute children.

A workhouse governor was employed with his wife as matron. The rest of the staff, cooks, nurses, cleaners, etc., were recruited from the workhouse inhabitants.

BOLTON CHRONICLE 22nd May 1852
BOARD OF GUARDIANS
Workhouse Dietary
"A report was read from the Workhouse Committee recommending the adoption by the Board of a dietary table for the able-bodied poor in the workhouses, according to which table food would be supplied to paupers as follows:
Breakfast for men and women, every day of the week
       4 oz. of Bread and 1½ pints milk porridge

Supper	every day for the week
	for men 2¼ lbs Oatmeal porridge and ¾ pint of milk.
	for women 2-lbs Oatmeal porridge and ¾ pint of milk.
Dinner	for men and women
Sunday	6 oz bread, 2 oz cheese, 1 pt coffee
Monday	3 oz bread, 4 oz beef, 1-lb potatoes, 1 pt broth.
Tuesday	6 oz bread, 1 pt coffee, ½ oz butter.
Wednesday	5 oz bread and 1½ pints rice milk.
Thursday	5 oz bread and 1½ pints pea soup.
Friday	1½-lbs suet pudding with sweetened butter.
Saturday	6 oz bread, one pint coffee and ½ oz butter."

BOLTON CHRONICLE 16th March 1853
"BOARD OF GUARDIANS
Dietary for children under 9 years of age
Breakfast	Bread and milk porridge as normal.
Dinner	Suet pudding three times a week
	Cooked meat with veg and bread twice a week.
	Coffee with bread and butter twice a week.
Supper	Milk porridge for those over 4 years of age,
	and for those under 4 years of age a sufficient quantity of bread and new milk.

Adopted with exception of new milk which was substituted by the Guardians to blue milk."

The question of providing work for the able-bodied paupers caused problems, particularly during the period of mass unemployment and poverty in 1855.

BOLTON CHRONICLE 24th February 1855
"BOARD OF GUARDIANS
By article 6 of the general order of the Poor Law Board of 14th December 1852, regulating the administration of relief, the guardians could not offer relief to able-bodied paupers, except in exchange for work. This morning he (Mr. Winder) understood they had sent fifty for employment to the workhouse while there was only room for two. It was, therefore, impossible to comply with that article under present conditions. Mr. Winder then suggested that the following resolution should be adopted:

> That the Poor Law Board be requested to suspend article 6 of the general order of the 14th December 1852, so far as regards the Bolton Union, for three months."

There was no sympathy from the Poor Law Board for the problems of the Bolton Union, and they replied that they (the

Poor Law Board) did not think that there was any absolute necessity for their suspending the provisions of the general relief order, and would not, therefore, feel justified in doing so.

The Board of Guardians then made efforts to comply with the work requirements.

BOLTON CHRONICLE 10th March
"BOARD OF GUARDIANS
A report was read from Mr. Best and Mr. Nicholson stating that in compliance with the wishes of the Workhouse Committee they had inspected the premises situated in the Shambles belonging to Mr. Thomas Baron, and they recommended the Board to take a few rooms there (the rental being 7s weekly) and that the same be fitted for the immediate reception of able-bodied paupers to be employed in picking oakum. Mr. Brown urged attention to that part of the report recommending the guardians to endeavour to provide work for the able-bodied out-door poor in their respective townships. He entirely disapproved of oakum picking as a labour test on the grounds that it was a serious loss.

The guardians gave 18s a cwt for the oakum, a man picked but 3-lbs a day for which he received a shilling, it consequently took him 37 days to pick 1 cwt, and the cost of his labour added to the price was £2. 15s, whereas they sold the oakum for 27s and thus lost 28s upon every cwt. This was independent of the loss in picking which the Governor stated to be between 20 and 50-lbs per cwt.

Mr. Nicholson was of the opinion that oakum picking was as good and effective a test as they could procure, pauper labour they could not render profitable, and they must therefore be prepared for a loss upon it. He recommended the taking of the room in the Shambles."

(Oakum picking – the pauper was supplied with a set amount of old ship's rope which was saturated in tar and hard as wood. This had to be shredded by hand into pieces small enough to be used to caulk ship's timbers.)

Whatever work was assigned to the able-bodied pauper the required amount had to be completed before relief was given. This too caused problems in the extreme conditions of 1855.

BOLTON CHRONICLE 3rd March 1855
"BOARD OF GUARDIANS
The Report (of the Workhouse Committee) also contained a recommendation that dinners be given to the able-bodied men sent for work at the house during the present distress, such a step being deemed advisable from the fact that many of the people remain

without food while at work during the whole day.

Mr. Hodson did not think there was very much wisdom in giving a meal to each of the able-bodied men sent to work at the workhouse. He also thought it would interfere very materially with the arrangements of the house, and for his own part would rather give the men 1s 6d a day than 1s and cook for them. He never liked opposing the recommendations of a Committee, but in this instance felt bound to do so.

Mr. Nicholson defended the course pursued by the Committee. At a time like this when people were actually starving to death the Guardians ought to relax the stringent rules by which they were guided in ordinary times.

Mr. Davies remarked that the amount proposed to be given in the shape of dinners was really so small as to excite his surprise that members of the board should be found to oppose it. They talked about the stringent laws of the Poor Law Board, and yet at the first opportunity they had of relaxing any themselves they refused to do so.

The question (of providing dinners) was put to the vote, when the amendment was carried by 12 to 8; the dinners will consequently not be allowed."

In more ordinary times the vagrant poor, no doubt classed as undeserving, received little sympathy, and not even the intervention of the Poor Law Board evoked any change of attitude.

BOLTON CHRONICLE 2nd November 1850
"BOARD OF GUARDIANS
A report was read from the Workhouse Committee on the subject of a communication from the Poor Law Board desiring the Guardians to provide proper covering for the beds in the vagrants' ward, knives and forks for the use of the inmates, and task work for the vagrants in return for what they received.

A report from the Tramp Master stated that the average number of vagrants taken into the tramp wards is 114 per week, and the expense is about 2s. 6d per week for fuel and brushes for cleaning, no food of any kind being given.

In reply to the letter of the Poor Law Board the Committee refer to their answers of the 13th May and 12th June last, stating the reasons why the Guardians do not provide covering for the vagrants, and with regard to task work, the Committee state that the yard at the workhouse being of limited extent the wishes of the Poor Law Board cannot be complied with at present.

Mr. Howarth and Mr. Entwistle thought that covering ought to be provided during the winter season. Mr. Hodson said that if they did find covering it would often be destroyed and the filth of the parties would engender disease.

The Clerk said he saw some poor Irish coming into the town the other night in a sad state of destitution. It was raining heavily at the time and they were almost naked. Now these unfortunate beings would no doubt have to go to the tramp house, where, very likely without food, they would have to sleep upon boards in their wet rags and without covering.

Mr. Entwistle said that they ought to give everyone a covering, and then they could take off their clothes and roll themselves in the quilt which would keep them off the hardboards. They gave the poor creatures nothing to eat, and this, in his opinion, was the very least that common humanity would dictate.

Mr. Nuttall said that such persons as the Clerk described went out begging in that condition to excite sympathy.

The Chairman (W. Scott, Esq) said the Irish were accustomed to go without shoes, even in the depth of winter, so that it was no hardship to them in that condition.

The amendment to refer the matter back to the workhouse Committee was defeated 9 to 8."

Not only were the Guardians unsympathetic to the vagrants arriving at the Workhouse gates; they were equally concerned that charity should not be rendered by sympathetic members of the public, and to discourage such compassion issued the following notice:

BOLTON CHRONICLE 11th January 1851
"BOLTON UNION
SUPPRESSION OF VAGRANCY, BEGGING, ETC.
The Board of Guardians beg leave to draw the attention of the Ratepayers and Inhabitants of all townships and places in the Union, to the great increase in the number of casual poor, consisting of Vagrants and Common Beggars, who spend their time in begging and plunder, and traverse the country in every direction, to the great prejudice of the industrious poor.

The relief afforded to such persons in the entire absence of any effectual inquiry into their habits or course of life, holds out great encouragement to sturdy beggars and vagabonds who prefer a life of idleness and vice to honest industry.

The law has provided that every person apparently destitute should be supplied with food and shelter, and at the cost of the Ratepayers. Relieving Officers have been appointed whose entire time is required to be devoted to the purpose of examining and, if really needed, administering relief to such persons, but the

Guardians and their officers feel it to be impossible without the aid and co-operation of the Ratepayers to carry out relief which shall discriminate between the really necessitous and the impostor, so long as humane but mistaken persons tolerate and encourage the system of begging from door to door. Convinced that the evil may, by the exercise of firmness and resolution, be eradicated and the inhabitants relieved from the annoyance and danger attendant on such visitations, the Guardians beg most strongly to suggest and urge all APPLICATIONS FOR ALL CHARITABLE AID BY BEGGARS AND WAYFARERS SHOULD BE REJECTED AND THE APPLICANT REFERRED TO THE RELIEVING OFFICER OF THE DISTRICT, who is instructed and required by law to investigate and in exercise of the discretion vested in him, to relieve or reject relief, in such cases as the circumstances may appear to him to require.

In furtherance of the course of procedure thus recommended the Guardians deem it important that each Ratepayer should be furnished with tickets imprinted with the name of the District Relieving Officer, and should present to each applicant one of such tickets referring his case to the officer. Tickets of the description alluded to have been prepared and may be had by any Ratepayer or Inhabitant on application to the Relieving Officer of his district."

So much for the 'undeserving' poor, and the inference of more concern for the 'deserving', or, as the Guardians name them, 'industrious' poor. The following report hardly reflects a more humane attitude to such deserving cases:

BOLTON CHRONICLE 6th September 1857
"BOARD OF GUARDIANS
Mr. Hulton drew attention to the case of a poor man which came under his notice a few days ago as he was driving through the town. His attention was attracted by the man's sickly appearance, and he was led in consequence to ask him his name and circumstances. The man stated his name was O'Brien, that he had been in the Queen's service in the Crimea, and that from lying in the trenches and being otherwise exposed to the inclemency of the weather his health had been completely broken down. He was living in a lodging house in Blackhorse Street in this town, his only income being a pension of 6d per day for six days a week. The man was unable to work and appeared very ill. From enquiries since made by the police at his (Mr. Hulton's) request he found that the man bore a good ordinary character, and the case seemed to be one of those deserving ones in which the Guardians might not improperly come forward and offer some assistance.

Mr. Green said he admired the philanthropic motive which

induced Mr. Hulton to bring this case under their notice, but he thought the guardians of Great Bolton had already sufficient to look after without their going to seek other cases, and as a dispenser of the public money he should oppose anything of the sort.

The Chairman said that if the man came to him he would give him a recommend for the Dispensary.

Mr. Green said he should of course not object to letting the man have a doctor, but what he disapproved of was their going about to seek cases.

Mr. Skelton having promised to inquire into the case the matter dropped."

Every effort to improve the conditions of those existing within the workhouse walls, whether made by individual guardians or the Poor Law Board Inspector, was invariably defeated by the majority of intransigent guardians, whether it be the education of pauper children, improved dietary, Christmas treat, or any other departure from the existing stringent conditions.

The case of the 'Christmas treat' exemplifies the attitude of the majority of these elected gentlemen of Bolton:

BOLTON CHRONICLE 26th December 1857
"REFUSAL OF THE USUAL CHRISTMAS TREAT TO THE WORKHOUSE INMATES

The Chairman, in moving the resolution of which he gave notice last week, that the inmates of both workhouses be treated to roast beef and plum pudding as usual on Christmas Day, said that he was sorry there was to be so much opposition to it, as he had been told there would be.

Mr. Cooper, the Assistant Clerk, had prepared a statement of the probable cost, with the proportion each township would have to contribute. From this it would appear that the total cost would be £21. 3s. 5d, of which some townships would have to contribute only 11d, and other who had no inmates in the workhouse, nothing. In the amount stated credit was not taken for food left, which would be used on the following day, thus reducing the amount by about £2, and if they made allowance also for the saving of the usual dinner, the actual cost would probably be reduced to £17. Mr. Latham begged to move that the inmates of both workhouses have their usual Christmas treat.

Mr. Alderman Dunderdale seconded the motion.

Mr. Nuttall opposed it and thought that Great Bolton had already enough to do without incurring this extra expenditure. The Vice-Chairman moved that no such dinner or provision take place.

He could never support the inmates of the workhouses being thus feasted while people outside were starving. It was really enough to send them to the workhouse.

Mr. Taylor said he could not vote for the motion while there was so much distress outside. It was true it might only be a small trifle which some of the townships would have to contribute, but in the aggregate it would amount to a great sum.

Mr. Brown supported the motion; it was only once a year they had the opportunity of giving these poor people a treat, and the poorest outside hardly ever passed over a year without a luxury of some sort.

The Vice-Chairman – Well, if they have it at their own expense let them have it.

Mr. Brown continued – Those inside the workhouse had no luxuries. The Guardians had it in their power to give them a luxury once a year. Many children in the workhouse were orphans, it was their misfortune to be there. Many too were widows, and it was their misfortune to be there, and because it was their misfortune were they to be deprived of that little Christmas cheer they had been accustomed to receive. He hoped not. They could let them have this treat now according to law, but not at any other time, why then should they be so parsimonious as to refuse it, when it would cost so little.

Mr. Brearley said he could not vote for the motion. He thought they should be just before they were generous out of the public purse. There were hundreds starving outside the workhouse who would be glad of beef and bread, let alone plum pudding, and if they did treat them he would rather the Guardians did it out of their own pocket and for that purpose he was willing to give £2. He was no advocate for eating and drinking out of the public purse.

Mr. Skelton said he should be very glad if the poor people could have a treat but he was afraid that by giving them one the Guardians committed a very great mistake. He believed that on the day it was proposed to give the workhouse inmates these plum puddings, hundreds if not thousands of people in the Union would not have common and ordinary food.

Mr. Hopwood said that he must say 'ditto' to almost all Mr. Skelton had said. Mr. Brown had gone too far when he laid so much stress upon the fatherless and widows.

Mr. Brown – Fact.

Mr. Hopwood – It is a fact likewise that three fourths of the people in the workhouse are rogues and vagabonds and only one fourth persons of good character.

Mr. Hodson said that he could not let such an assertion pass unnoticed. The Governor told him that morning that there was not one able-bodied man in either establishment. He sympathised with the poor old creatures and also with the widows and orphans, and while he studied, as he ever did, the interests of the rate-payers, he would not deprive the poor people of the usual Christmas cheer. He trusted that no member of the Board would lack the spirit of humanity to deny it.

Mr. Skelton – It is humanity to the payers.

The Chairman said the bulk of them were old and infirm and then there were the children. He was an advocate of economy, but would bear his share of the responsibility in allowing the people this treat.

The question was then put, when the amendment was carried by 13 against 9.

Mr. Hodson – I am sorry for that. The treat will, therefore, not be given."

The following week the Bolton Chronicle was able to report that the workhouse inmates would, after all, receive their treat.

Captain Gray, one of Bolton's Members of Parliament, having heard of the Board's decision, had communicated to the Board his willingness to pay the full cost himself. The Board thereupon agreed that if the treat was to cost the Union nothing they could have it.

The matter of the education of children in the workhouse also received the same negative and obstructive attitude. In May 1855 the Inspector of Schools had visited the Workhouse and made the following report.

"I have examined the children in the workhouse. Out of 31 present, 3 only were able to read and all were in a state of extreme ignorance. One girl only could write her name, and none could work a sum of any kind. This workhouse is evidently a very improper place for children. I earnestly hope that something more effectual may be done by the Guardians for the education of the destitute in this populous union. Turton can admit few of those who require moral and religious training, and who, as it is to be feared, are not likely to be rescued from vice and crime by any but the Guardians."

This adverse report was followed by a letter from Mr. Farnall, Poor Law Inspector, who required to know what effect had been given to the provisions of the Act of 1834, enabling the Guardians to educate the children of poor persons in receipt of outdoor relief.

At the meeting of the Board of Guardians at which the letter was read, Mr. Hopwood said the plan of which he most approved was that everybody should educate their own. The education of children whose parents were receiving outdoor relief would prove very expensive, and in his opinion was foreign to the object for which the Board of Guardians was formed.

The Board resolved that Mr. Farnell should be informed that they had not taken any steps in the matter.

Not surprisingly the indifference and cynical attitude resulted in a scathing denouncement of certain Guardians in the Editorial letter of the 15th June 1855.

> "We are ashamed to record the absurdities and worse into which the proceedings forced some members of the Board. For instance take Mr. Sylvester's extraordinary notions of the limits which should be put to the aspirations of an honest soul born to the oppression of a ragged jacket – "The children of the workhouse were educated to a certain extent and he thought quite as much as paupers *had a right to expect*." Let us thank God that Mr. Sylvester holds not unchecked the iron rod of so fearfully narrow a prejudice over all the poverty and misfortune of Bolton. Strangely enough there were others found to think as Mr. Sylvester "thought", even to the quality and quantity of heaven's mercy which paupers "had right to expect".
>
> Mr. Hodson proposed the adjournment of the matter for twelve months, though he had no objection to "furnishing" the children with – "education, so far as reading of the Bible, or something in a similar way."
>
> It is a sad and dangerous doctrine to broach that poverty deserves neither care nor consideration; that it is a thing to be despised and to be sneered at, to be left alike without hope and without consolation; for what else does Mr. Sylvester teach?"

Gradually over the years a more liberal and sympathetic attitude did prevail, and two teachers were appointed at Turton Workhouse, and the efforts of Mr. P. R. Arrowsmith, J.P., in establishing an Industrial Ragged School in Bolton, did much to alleviate the apathetic attitude to the education of the poor and destitute children of the town.

The great bone of contention which was thrown regularly before the Guardians to growl and snarl over was the question of providing a new workhouse. The inadequacy of the Fletcher Street buildings was never contradicted, but the spending of the ratepayers' money on new and proper accommodation for

The Poor

the paupers was bitterly opposed. Complaints from the Poor Law Board Inspector resulted in the ruthless pruning of the inmates, in an attempt to justify the adequacy of the existing buildings. After years of procrastination a Committee was appointed in 1853 to consider and report on the necessity of erecting a new workhouse. This committee laid before the Board of Guardians the following report:

> "The present house is calculated to accommodate 353 inmates. It is not well adapted for that number, nor even for a smaller number, in consequence of there being no means of preserving order in it.
>
> From the want of proper accommodation there cannot be the necessary classification of the inmates, and for want of this, it is calculated to increase pauperism rather than to decrease it, because of the coming together of the indolent, the vicious and the young. It is at present scarcely possible to keep the sexes apart, and at times not possible.
>
> The present dining room has only one door into it and the room itself is too small for more than 100 inmates. This causes great confusion, some paupers with their children come to the house and live there for a time and yet never once enter the dining room at meal times, much food is consequently carried to various rooms and it is almost impossible to prevent a greater number of meals being carried out than ought to be. Church service is daily read in the dining room, but for want of sufficient room many unruly inmates never come to hear it. Owing to the construction of the present House there are too many opportunities for the sexes to meet and there is too much sight seeing. If such was not the case and if the House could be rendered more irksome to young persons by taking away the above opportunities, particularly as regards females, the tendency would be to lessen pauperism. In respect of the hospital it is quite full, not having room for one patient more. The fever ward has been half full but is not so now. The present buildings are scarcely capable, at any expense, of being so changed as to answer the purposes well for which they are now used."

That was in 1853, but it was 27th September 1856 before the Bolton Chronicle could report any material progress and that progress still marred by bickering.

BOLTON CHRONICLE *27th September 1856*
"PROPOSED NEW WORKHOUSE
After a discussion extending more or less over the past 10 years the Guardians of this Union, in January of the present year, passed a resolution that the present Bolton Workhouse being inadequate a

new one be erected forthwith, the Board at the same time forming itself into a Committee to carry the same into effect. No one at all conversant with the real facts of the case would question the wisdom of that decision. . . .

Over and over again have the defects of the establishment been pointed out by the Poor Law Inspectors and others, but the Guardians scouted the very mention of a new workhouse and preferred laying out money in the patching up of a building which, as the event has proved, never could be suitable to the purpose to which it was devoted. Gradually, however, though slowly, the feeling began to gain ground that the present house could not much longer serve the requirements of a district daily extending itself in numbers, and the question of a new workhouse was revived with new vigour. After innumerable and protracted discussions, the perusal of which in our columns week after week must have sorely taxed the patience of our readers, an important step towards the long desired end was made in October last, when the Board decided that the workhouse accommodation on the Union was inadequate to its wants. On the 28th of the following month a return was called for, on the motion of Mr. Birley, showing the amount of money expended on the two workhouses for alterations, repairs, additions and improvements from the 25th March 1847 to the 25th March 1855. That return showed that no less a sum than £4,435 had been laid out on Bolton Workhouse and £1,141. 19. 6d on the establishment at Turton, making a total on the two houses of £5,576 19. 6d. Since then little has been spent on them, the feeling evidently being that it would be wiser to spend the money on the erection of a new establishment.

Eight months have elapsed since the Board resolved to build a workhouse *forthwith*, and yet they have not yet been able to agree as to the precise spot on which it shall stand. Various sites have been proposed, but we cannot say they have all been discussed upon their merits, and though the selection after a while became narrowed to three – two of which were in turn chosen and rejected – it soon became evident that none of them could be carried, such was the ill-feeling and animosity which had been engendered during the time they were under consideration.

Other tenders were sent in and after the Guardians had visited the sites then offered – only one of which had been previously before the board – two of them were rejected at once as unsuitable and from the remaining two, the one at Fishpool in Farnworth, and the other on Deane Moor belonging to Henry Tempest, Esq., it was determined to select the site on which should stand the future workhouse of this Union. That at Fishpool was generally approved – a Committee of the whole Board meeting on the ground, when 21 out of 25 present voted for it and none against.

At the meeting of the Board, however, on Wednesday last, as if in total oblivion of the unanimity of the Friday's proceedings, objections were started to the site newly chosen, by those who, so far from opposing it then, actually supported it.

Ultimately it was decided to take the site selected and to purchase the land (16½ statute acres) at £140 per acre, but there was still so much diversity of opinion as to the relative merits of the two sites on the Fishpool estates, that Mr. Farnall, the Poor Law Inspector, is now to be invited to inspect them and having selected that which he deems best a motion stands on the book pledging the Board to abide by his decision, and to rescind the resolution in favour of the site already selected should Mr. Farnall report against it. But will the Board pledge itself to adhere to that gentleman's choice? Really Messrs Guardians, is it not time to decide?"

In the midst of all this disagreement and bitterness the inadequacy of the accommodation in the existing workhouse was again tragically underlined, when on 3rd May 1857, Isabella Longworth, aged 70, a pauper inmate, was attacked by a lunatic named Nancy Horrocks, and died from the injuries received. The post mortem revealed that the deceased had six ribs fractured on the right side and five ribs fractured on the left side. Dr. Chadwick who conducted the examination considered that had the injuries not been inflicted Isabella Longworth would still be alive, and attributed her death to internal injuries, produced by external violence. The Inquest Jury agreed upon a verdict of "Wilful murder" against Nancy Horrocks, who was detained pending trial at the next Liverpool Assizes.

The Bolton Chronicle campaigned for a public inquiry into the circumstances leading up to the death of Isabella Longworth, and was delighted to report on 16th May 1857 that the Board of Guardians had agreed to such an investigation. The delight was short lived, as the editorial of the 30th May 1857 reveals:

"THE LATE DEATH BY VIOLENCE AT THE WORKHOUSE
We regret to find from the proceedings at the last meeting of the Board of Guardians, that there is to be no further inquiry to be made into the circumstances connected with the death of Isabella Longworth at the Bolton Workhouse.

The Poor Law Board appear to treat the matter lightly, making it merely the subject of a caution to the Master and Matron, as well as to the nurse of the female lunatics. We still adhere to the opinion that a full and searching investigation into the whole facts of the case ought to have been instituted. It is most probable that no blame attaches to any particular person in connection with this liability, but there must be something wrong about a system which allows of the possibility of such a melancholy result as that upon which we are commenting. We have a strong conviction that if a careful and sufficient examination had been made, it would have been apparent that the present workhouse and its arrangements are miserably inadequate for the accommodation of the very large numbers of insane persons confined there."

By 1858 all had been resolved and the corner stone of the new Bolton Workhouse was laid at Fishpool, Farnworth.

BOLTON CHRONICLE 11th September 1858
"LAYING OF THE CORNER STONE OF THE BOLTON UNION WORKHOUSE
The ceremony of the laying of the corner stone of the new Bolton Union Workhouse took place on Wednesday 8th September 1858. We have but little data as to what were the workhouse requirements or what the workhouse provision of this parish was in former days, but they were doubtless small even in comparison with the then limited population. We find that at the close of the last century the present Three Arrows Public House in Oldhall Street was used as a poor house, which doubtless served for both Great and Little Bolton. This seems to have been found sufficient for the requirements of the two townships until the year 1810, in the early part of which we find from the records of the old trustees, whose meetings were held at the Queen Anne Session Rooms, it was resolved to erect the present workhouse in Fletcher Street.

In 1837 the Bolton Poor-law Union was established and this involved Great and Little Bolton and 24 other townships. In 1839 the Guardians became the tenants of the workhouse at Turton.

Humphrey Cheetham, who resided at Turton Tower, having regard to the claims of the poor of Turton, bequeathed the farm at Goose-coat Hill, the rents of which have been annually expended by the trustees in the purchase of clothing for the poor. The original farmhouse was found to be so commodious as to become the nucleus of the House of Industry and by successive enlargements it reached the premises comprising Turton Workhouse."

Even the laying of the corner stone brought forth caustic comment from one spectator whose letter to the editor was

The new Bolton Union Workhouse (*Bolton Almanac*)

published in the Bolton Chronicle. The letter was headed "The Free Fuddle at Fishwick", and goes on to say –

> "The discussions relating to the building have been in all conscience disgraceful enough, without making such a finish as was exhibited last Wednesday.
> Perhaps the most disgusting feature of the affair on the part of several guardians is that the alleged motive for their swilling so much liquor was "to make it cost the Chairman a pretty penny", and they talk about the improvidence, dissolute and intemperate habits of the working classes."

Perhaps that is a suitable epitaph on which to conclude this chapter on the Bolton Board of Guardians of the Poor.

CRIME AND PUNISHMENT

The Law was applied with the moral and zealous fervour of most Victorian endeavours. Numerous commissions considered and pronounced on the application of the law, on prisons, and on punishments. Hanging was preserved from 1836 for the murderer; other crimes were punished by transportation, imprisonment or fines. In the 1840's there had been a vast project of building new prisons, and various systems of dealing with offenders were tried. The old type of filthy prisons, mostly corruptly administered, were replaced with strictly regimented places of confinement. Enforced silence, the treadmill, the crank, shot-drill, were introduced to induce reformation of the criminal – which was, in many cases, successful in that after serving a lengthy term of such imprisonment the offender was in no physical or mental condition to undertake any further criminal activity.

Through the objections of several Australian States at being used as dumping ground for English criminals, the sentence of transportation was beginning to be phased out and a sentence of "penal servitude" substituted. At the South Lancashire Assizes on 15th August 1853 Judge Baron Watson thought fit to explain the position and said:

> "The old sentence of transportation is entirely abolished and we have now introduced for the same term of years as in the case of transportation, the punishment of penal servitude. One where they may be sent to foreign countries, or may be kept in this country; but they will be kept as slaves, doomed to labour all that period of time, and it must never go abroad for one instant that the punishment is lessened by using the words 'penal servitude' instead of that of 'transportation'."

The sanctity of "property" was emphasised in the application of the Law. Concessions were made to the right of an individual to injure another – providing you stopped short of murder – but beware if you purloined his goods or harmed his property. The following cases typify this attitude.

BOLTON CHRONICLE 6th April 1850
"BOLTON QUARTER SESSIONS
Richard Kirkman, 13, and James Pickup, 12, pleaded guilty of stealing on the 4th February ten pieces of iron, etc., the property of Richard Crook.
Kirkman, 6 months, last fourteen days solitary confinement and whipped.
Pickup, 3 months and whipped."

"BOLTON BOROUGH COURT
On Thursday last at the Borough Court a charge was preferred against a young man named Jeremiah Pendlebury, a piecer, of committing an indecent assault upon Sarah Ann Darbishire, aged 6 years and 4 months. The child, an intelligent looking girl, was the daughter of a person, who, being deprived of sight is known as "Blind James", residing at the Flags, Churchgate. Pendlebury had been in the habit of visiting the blind man's residence, and according to the child's statement had committed the offence charged. It was alleged that he had communicated to her a loathsome disorder, which was corroborated by evidence given by Mr. Snape, Surgeon.
The prisoner was fined £5, in default to be committed for two months."

At the same Quarter Sessions, Ann Haslam, aged 42, was indicted for stealing two candlesticks, the property of John Hardman. The sentence for that offence was "transported for 7 years."

BOLTON CHRONICLE 2nd April 1853
"BOLTON BOROUGH SESSIONS
Jane Gallagher, aged 15 years, pleaded guilty to stealing a shawl belonging to Jane Lomax. Sentenced to twelve months imprisonment.
Edward Beardsworth, aged 24 years, was found guilty of stealing on the 29th October, two pair of clog tops and four pieces of leather belonging to George Bradshaw.
Seven years transportation.
Joseph Greenwood, 16 years, for stealing a handkerchief from the person of William Bradley was sentenced to six months imprisonment.

Jonathan Barber, for manslaughter in killing his wife, six calendar months imprisonment with hard labour.
William Christy, for manslaughter, eighteen months imprisonment with hard labour."

On a lighter note, the Bolton Chronicle reported on 25th November 1854 –

"A CANDIDATE FOR THE WAR
At the Borough Court on Monday, 20th December a half-famished looking fellow, who gave his name as George Thompson, and said he was 26 years of age, was brought up under the following circumstances. About twenty minutes to twelve on Saturday night, he went to the Police office and said he wanted to be locked up; he had nowhere to go, and had in vain tried to enlist for all the recruiting party were drunk. The Police-officer at the lock-ups gave him to understand however, that he could not be locked-up in absence of a charge; and the man accordingly left, went right away to a shop in Mealhouse-lane and got two pies for which he refused to pay, saying he wanted to be sent off either to the army or the navy. A police officer was accordingly sent for, and he was then locked up. When brought before the bench he was still of the same opinion, saying that to be killed in fighting "th' Rooshans" was preferable to being "clemmed to't death". The Magistrates were unwilling to prevent his services being available in so praiseworthy a cause, and accordingly liberated him; when he left the Court he met with a Recruiting Sergeant and joyfully accepted the shilling."

BOLTON CHRONICLE *24th December 1852*
"BRUTAL ASSAULT ON POLICE
Thomas Glynn, 41, and Edward Lyons, 22, were indicted for a most brutal and unmanly assault upon Robert Murray and other police-constables, whilst in the execution of their duty on the 11th inst. The Recorder said that if the police were not supported in the execution of their duties, it was impossible to preserve the peace of the town. Lyons seemed to have originated the disturbance and he was sentenced to nine months and Glynn to three months imprisonment."

"STEALING BUTTER
Agnes Mann, a female, aged 60 years, was indicted for stealing 7 lb of butter from the shop of Mr. Thomas Stewart, grocer, Deansgate on the 2nd inst. She was found guilty. A person in court stepped forward and pleaded in favour of the old woman, that since sustaining a domestic calamity some time ago she had been subject

to mental aberrations of the most distressing kind.
She was sentenced to be imprisoned and kept to hard labour for four months."

Bolton had at least taken advantage of the Act of Parliament which permitted the raising and equipping of a professional Police Force, to fight the growing incidence of crime. The fact that they had such a force is complimentary, when it is considered that in 1853 twenty two counties had made no attempt to implement the recommendations of the Act, and still relied on the locally elected constable. A further Act in 1856 made the raising of a professional force obligatory.

In 1851 Bolton's Police Force consisted of a Superintendent, 4 Sergeants, 13 first class and 7 second class constables, and the total cost of maintaining this force, including clothing, for the year, amounted to £1,397 4s. 4d.

During the year they arrested 2,839 persons, of which 1,453 were summarily convicted, and 1,250 discharged. The remaining 136 were committed for trial, of which number 24 were sentenced to transportation, 94 imprisoned, 17 acquitted and one was not yet tried.

Statistics were avidly collected, and it was shown that of the persons apprehended 2,175 were English and Welsh; 644 were Irish, and 20 were Scots; and further 412 could neither read nor write; 2,405 could read or write imperfectly, and only 22 could read and write well.

As with poverty and drunkenness there was beginning to be an awareness of the cause of much of the crime that abounded.

The futility of whipping and imprisoning children for stealing, and then returning them to an environment in which they could only manage a precarious survival on what they could beg or steal, was beginning to be appreciated.

BOLTON CHRONICLE 13th July 1850
"JUVENILE MENDICITY IN BOLTON
Under this title Mr. P. R. Arrowsmith has published a letter addressed to the Mayor, suggesting the establishment of a "Ragged School" (under some other name) in the Borough, with a view to relieve our town from the danger, dishonour, the cost of permitting the children of the very poor, or the very depraved, to be bred in our streets to the practice of begging and pilfering.

The general plan of these schools will be pretty well known by this time, it is not only to teach the children, but that they may be induced to attend school, to feed them also, the latter being an absolute necessary condition, as you can no more hope to instruct a starving child than you can keep it from stealing for food, unless you provide it with sustenance honestly got. By the aid of Mr. Harris, Superintendent of Police, Mr. Arrowsmith is enabled to show that two hundred young persons are known to the police (in this town) as beggars or thieves under training, that during the past ten years there have been 507 apprehensions of children under 14 years of age, 435 of whom were totally uneducated, and concludes by an urgent appeal to the inhabitants to step in between the children of the Borough, now known to be growing up in crime and bestial ignorance, not alone to save our taxes and our property, not alone to make them useful members of an industrial community, not alone to save them from crime and punishment in this life, but to save them from spiritual death in the world to come."

A few years were to pass before Mr. Arrowsmith's dream became a reality. In 1853 Mr. Arrowsmith again brought the matter up in Council:

BOLTON CHRONICLE 30th July 1853
"COUNCIL PROCEEDINGS
REFORMATORY SCHOOLS
Mr. P. R. Arrowsmith begged with the permission of the Mayor and Council to offer some remarks on a subject not named in the notice paper. He said that there was now before Parliament a bill for the purpose of providing that which every magistrate had, in the exercise of his duty, felt to be one of the greatest desiderations in Society, namely, the establishment of reformatory schools. He believed the great proportion of the time of every Magistrate was taken up in trying offences of children, and instead of sending them to prison to learn the business of crime more perfectly, to be hardened and trained by older hands to become more accomplished in their calling, this bill had the very humane and laudable object of providing schools for the reformation of such criminals. It further provided that – "if any child found wandering abroad, not having any home or settled place of abode, nor any lawful or visible means of subsistence other than the begging of alms, and not being able to give a satisfactory account of himself or herself be brought by any constable or peace officer before the Justices, they may require such child to find a sufficient surety for his or her good behaviour, or in default be sent to such reformatory school for such period as may seem necessary."

Mr. Arrowsmith said that it had long been felt by the Bolton, and every other, bench of Justices that some measure was necessary for dealing with this, the most dangerous class of the community, and he thought every member of the Council would support him in taking the step he had to propose.

He moved the adoption of the following petition, that it should be signed by the Mayor, sealed with the corporate seal, and transmitted to T. Barnes, Esq., M.P. for presentation:

To the honourable, the Commons of the United Kingdom of Great Britain and Ireland, in parliament assembled.

The humble petition of the Mayor, Aldermen and Burgesses of the Borough of Bolton, in Council assembled, sheweth that your petitioners highly approving of the provisions of a bill now before your honourable house entitled "A bill for the better care and reformation of juvenile offenders", and believing that its operations, if carried into effect, will tend greatly to the benefit of the community at large, earnestly pray that the bill may be passed into law.

The proposition was put and carried unanimously."

By the end of the year Mr. Arrowsmith had himself been elected Mayor, and in anticipation of the will of Parliament, seized the chance to further his ideals and called a public meeting.

BOLTON CHRONICLE *31st December 1853*
"BOLTON INDUSTRIAL RAGGED SCHOOL
At an influential preliminary meeting of the inhabitants of the Borough of Bolton and its neighbourhood, favourable to the establishment of an Industrial Ragged School, held at the Borough Court House on Wednesday, 28th December 1853, convened and presided over by
    Peter Rothwell Arrowsmith, Esq, Mayor
the following resolutions were unanimously passed:–
Moved by Robert Heywood, Esq.
Seconded by Thomas Ridgway Bridson, Esq.,
That in the opinion of this meeting a great amount of juvenile destitution, ignorance, vagrancy and crime has long existed in this Borough, for which no adequate remedy has yet been provided.
Moved by the Rev. Mr. Gridleston,
Seconded by the Rev. Mr. Kemp,
That it appears to this meeting that a large proportion of the present aggregate of crime might be prevented, and numbers of miserable human beings, who have nothing before them, under our present system, but a hopeless career of wickedness and vice, might be converted into virtuous, honest and industrious citizens, if due care were taken to rescue destitute, neglected and criminal children from the dangers and temptations incident to their

position.
Moved by William Gray, Esq.
Seconded by H. M. Richardson, Esq.,
That as the Ragged Industrial Schools existing in this Country have produced beneficial effects on the children of the most destitute classes of society inhabiting large towns, it is, therefore, desirable that a similar institution be established in this Borough."

A subscription list was opened and a Committee formed. The response was such that the total of £2,535 received enabled the Committee to buy suitable premises in Commission Street.

In April 1854 the Committee interviewed the seventeen applicants for the post of Master and Matron of the School, and ultimately selected Mr. Edward Couzens of the Moral and Industrial School, Leeds, and Miss Clarke of the same town.

The objects of the School were laid down as:

"To provide scriptural instruction and the rudiments of useful knowledge, together with industrial occupation of destitute children of both sexes, between the ages of seven and fourteen years, and particularly those who procure a precarious subsistence by pilfering and begging."

BOLTON CHRONICLE 24th June 1854
"The Bolton Industrial Ragged School was opened on Monday for the reception of those really needy children, whose preservation and reclamation from a life of poverty, vice and crime, this excellent institution is intended to promote."

BOLTON CHRONICLE 13th January 1855
CORRESPONDENCE
"To: The Editor of the Bolton Chronicle
An Appeal for the Ragged School
Dear Sir,

We have got an Industrial Ragged School, and I verily believe it to be what its name implies, for unless something more be done for these poor children, whose misfortune it is to be dependent upon such an institution, there will be very few bones left to carry the rags about this winter. I have for several mornings lately noticed two little girls apparently about 8 years old, going to school, without shoes, stockings, caps or bonnets, and scarcely any clothing upon them but an old frock each. Now imagine two children of the age before mentioned, having to go a quarter of a mile on such a morning as Wednesday week, with no covering but what I have stated, and judge whether after their arrival at school, perishing with cold, as we are positive they must have been, it would be impossible to expect them to be industrious or attentive when one of our most healthy adults would be scarcely able to do half-a-days work if compelled to walk through the snow barefooted, as these two little children were.

I am certain that there are gentlemen upon the Committee and subscribers to the school who have plenty of shoes and stockings, and different kinds of clothing, which they do not consider fit for their own children to wear and are therefore cast away as rags. If these gentlemen would place them at the disposal of the Master and Mistress of the above School, many of the sufferings of these poor children might be alleviated, if not entirely removed.

Hoping the above remarks will be taken into consideration,
I am, Sir,
HUMANITAS"

THE INDUSTRIOUS POOR

Whilst the preceding chapters have shown the consequences of a non-industrious existence, whether by choice or misfortune, what of the gainfully employed?

The Factory Act of 1833 had been of immense importance to a town so involved in the cotton trade. The Act directed that children under 9 years of age should not be employed, and that from then until their 14th year should not be employed more than 8 hours per day. Between 14 and 18 work was to be curtailed to not more than 69 hours per week.

Opponents of the Act considered that the cotton trade would be ruined. The loss of cheap child labour would lead to such high yarn prices that the majority of foreign trade would be lost, and the loss to families of the wages of their children would lead to escalating poverty, a view that was echoed by parents as well as the mill owners.

Sir George Phillips, M.P., the mill owner, claimed that delicate children were specifically sent to work in factories because they were delicate, and in factories they could be well clothed and warm. This seemingly outrageous suggestion did contain an element of truth, for the mines and the foundries were far worse environments for child labour.

This fact, plus the inclusion in the Act of the appointment of Government inspectors to ensure full adherence to the law, was the bitter pill which mill owners found hard to swallow. All previous Acts designed to regulate conditions and hours of work had not been backed up with such provisions, and were consequently taken little heed of. The new Act empowered Inspectors to enter a factory at any time; check the register of hours worked by each child; examine witnesses under oath, and even imprison recalcitrant witnesses for contempt.

Mill owners and their supporters had banded themselves into "The Factory Law Amendment Association", and on 21st

April 1855 the Bolton Chronicle reported a meeting of the 'factory owners of the United Kingdom' at which they complained of prejudice and ill will borne towards factory owners on the part of the community at large, and displayed in the contents of Dicken's "Household Words", and copied into the London morning papers.

> "Upwards of 2,000 accidents in factories, being the usual average, occurred in the half year last reported upon by the factory inspectors. Of this number all but about 100 were not only preventable, but such as mill owners are bound by law to prevent. It has been proved by the experience of mill owners who have obeyed the dictates of humanity that every part of the machinery they use can be securely fenced without producing the great fire of Manchester, or causing the total ruin of Great Britain as a manufacturing country. The Home Secretary has, therefore, since we last called attention to this subject, rescinded every compromise between right and convenience that was a year ago admitted by authority, and has ordered that henceforth the law shall be enforced to the utmost. Instantly a large number of mill owners fly to the platform, deliver and hear angry orations, form deputations, and declare themselves a slaughtered interest."

The mill owners in righteous indignation asked that attention be drawn to the enormous number of accidents in other trades. 985 deaths had occurred in coal mining last year, and the deaths in factories were only 42.

> "Why should the man at Wigan with a mine, or the iron owner in Staffordshire, or the tin miner in Cornwall, or the lead miner in Cumberland, hold up his head as a man carrying on his business in an honest and upright manner, when unfortunately 1,200 lives were sacrificed in those pursuits, whilst the mill owner was to be upbraided, despised and held up to public reprobation, when in a population of twice the number, and oft-times through the carelessness of the victims themselves, only 42 deaths had occurred."

The mill owners had a point, but the factory workers had strong and vigorous supporters, including some mill owners themselves, who were in a position to battle and force the Act through Parliament, whilst workers in other industries were not so fortunate.

The fears of 1833 that the cotton industry would decline as a result of the Act were completely unfounded; quite a few mill owners conceded that the loss of child labour and reduction in working hours had not resulted in a loss of production, but that shorter hours and better conditions had had the opposite effect on production.

There was continual expansion in the trade, and new factories were being built, and cotton operatives and their families were reaping some benefit from the increasing opportunity of employment.

Two events in the 1850's illustrated the changing climate of employment within the industry. The first demonstrates the effectiveness of the Factory Act in relation to the employee, and the second the effectiveness of the united strength of the operatives themselves.

BOLTON CHRONICLE 15th June 1850
"ACCIDENT BY MACHINERY
On Tuesday last, about 12 o'clock, an accident of a serious nature took place at the mill of Messrs Platt and Sutcliffe, Chew Moor, Lostock.

Nancy Coe, a girl aged 13 years, whilst sweeping a 'wheelgate' was caught by an upright shaft, the consequence of which was that she had her clothes torn from her body, and her arm taken off a little below the elbow. She was soon afterwards attended by Mr. A. Robinson and Mr. Garstang, Surgeons, when amputation was performed. The poor girl was also dreadfully bruised in many parts of her body. She at present lies in a very precarious state."

BOLTON CHRONICLE 21st August 1850
"FACTORY INFORMATION
At the County Sessions Room on Monday last, Messrs. Platt and Sutcliffe, Cotton Spinners, were summoned before the Magistrates, Rev. J. S. Birley and C. J. Darbishire and P. Martin, Esqs., on a charge of having offended against the Factory Act, 7 & 8 Vic., by neglecting to fence certain machinery in their mill at Lostock, in consequence of which Nancy Coe, a young person, suffered bodily injury on the 11th June.

The female Coe was engaged in sweeping when being caught by a shaft insufficiently fenced she had her right arm taken off. The mill was three storeys high and the accident occurred in the middle room in which were two new pairs of self-acting mules. One of the pairs of mules commenced working about 2nd June, but the other did not start till after the accident occurred, and it was while engaged in getting the machinery ready for starting that Coe received her injury. Nancy Coe stated that while engaged in sweeping she turned herself round when the shaft caught her frock and whizzed her round and she became insensible. When she came to herself her right arm was gone and her heel was cut. In cross examination she said she did not know previously to being caught that any part of the shaft was uncased. Since the accident Messrs. Platt and Sutcliffe had shown her every kindness by paying her wages and providing her with medical attention, clothes and refreshments. The Magistrates having retired and been absent for about half-an-hour returned into Court. Mr. Birley stated they considered an offence had been committed in the upright shaft not being securely fenced, and they should convict Messrs. Platt and Sutcliffe in the mitigated penalty of £10 and costs of 46s."

The case did not rest with this conviction, and extensive legal disputes ensued. The main point being contested was that the Act did not specify that 'upright shafts' be fenced.

In March 1851 the verdict was upheld at the Liverpool Assizes and Nancy Coe was awarded £120 damages. The judgment was arrested by the Court of the Exchequer in the following June. There was an appeal on behalf of Nancy Coe before Judges of the Queen's Bench and Common Pleas, who upheld the decision of the Court of the Exchequer. A further appeal was made before a special jury at the Liverpool Assizes in 1852. Mr. Justice Cresswell directed a verdict to be entered for Messrs. Platt and Sutcliffe, but leave was made for an application to be again made to the Court of the Exchequer. The case was fully argued in the Court of the Exchequer on 27th May 1852, and a written judgment was delivered by Mr. Baron Alderson. This judgment ruled that "The defendants (Platt and Sutcliffe) had not been negligent at common law, nor omitted anything required by law, that is to say they have not committed an offence. The rule, therefore, must be discharged."

Though Nancy Coe eventually lost her case, the significant factor is that the case was presented in the first place, and then fought on her behalf in the higher courts. The power of the Act and its implementation had been very strongly demonstrated.

In 1860 there was a 'demonstration' of a different nature, and Lostock was again in the news.

BOLTON CHRONICLE 8th September 1860
"IMPORTANT MEETING OF OPERATIVE COTTON SPINNERS
On Thursday evening a large meeting was held at the Club House,

Millstone Inn, Crown Street, at which were assembled delegates from 65 mills and representatives of every firm in the Borough and district.

The object of the meeting was stated to be:-

To take into consideration the most advisable means of enforcing the Bolton List of Prices for spinners at the new mill near Lostock Junction, Rumworth. It is the firm of Messrs. T. & J. Heaton, Halliwell, who formerly owned the Delph Hill Mill, better known by the name of Doffcocker Mill. It is a firm that would never pay the same prices as other masters for spinning, for previous to the Doffcocker Mill being burned down it can be proved that they were paying fifty per cent below the Masters of Bolton for spinning the same quality of yarns.

It was urged that the manner in which Mr. Joseph Heaton conducted himself towards the Association was such as that body could not, and would not, permit. The deputation stated that, when they asked if the rumour of underpaying was incorrect, the reply they obtained was "that he should pay such prices as he thought proper, and he wouldn't be dictated to by anyone, and wouldn't have a man in his employ who belonged to the Trade Union." A decision was unanimously come to "that the deputation again wait upon Messrs Heaton on the following morning and if they would not comply with the Bolton list, the deputation be authorised to empower the hands this week to give a fortnight's notice, and that no engagements be made to spin at the above firm until the Masters agree to the deputation's terms."

In accordance with the decision of the meeting the delegation again waited upon Messrs Heaton yesterday, and were courteously received.

After making known to them the results of the meeting the Masters replied that they paid by the same list of prices as Messrs Ormrod and Hardcastle on account of spinning the same quality of yarns. On being informed to the contrary Messrs Heaton promised to make enquiry into it, and on ascertaining the statement of the operatives to be correct agreed to rectify the matter.

Under these circumstances the men were ordered not to give notice, and there at present the matter rests."

The power of a 'union' had now been demonstrated, but again cotton operatives were fortunate in that 'spinners' were master craftsmen, who could not be replaced out of the hordes of unskilled unemployed, and their strength lay in that knowledge.

With the building of new mills a further benefit came the way of the operatives, in that in quite a few cases owners were also building houses for their workers alongside the mills. These terraced houses, whilst of no architectural beauty, provided clean and substantial homes, in marked contrast to the overcrowded, insanitary hovels in which so many other workers lived. There was also the enlightened owner who provided far more than just homes for his employees.

Robert Gardner, owner of Dean Mills at Barrow Bridge, was an outstanding example. He provided an Institute for recreation and education, a library with provincial and London papers, periodicals and books, facilities for meals and baths, a co-operative shop, and ovens for baking bread. Perhaps more remarkable in an age when there was still considerable religious intolerance, Gardner and his partner Bazley insisted that only basic Christianity be taught in the schools, and pupils were encouraged to follow their own conscience. They underlined their insistence by building neither church nor chapel in their community. Dean Mills became a focal point of attention and interest, and exemplified as practical proof that employer and employee could work together with substantial profit to both. The final accolade came with the visit of Prince Albert on 11th October 1851 when passing through Bolton.

BOLTON CHRONCILE 11th October 1851
"PRINCE ALBERT IN BOLTON AND HALLIWELL
His Royal Highness, Prince Albert, has this day passed through Bolton to and from Halliwell, and returned to Worsley to accompany Her Majesty homewards. The only visit of Royalty to Bolton of which we are at present enabled to speak with certainty, was that of Prince Rupert – the Prince having stormed and taken the town in the year 1644.

This morning work was universally suspended and at an early hour considerable numbers of people made their appearance in the streets, the carriage ways of which were kept clear by posts and ropes.

Along the whole line of road through which His Royal Highness had to pass viz: Deansgate, Bridge Street and St. George's Street, flags and banners, some of them of a beautiful and striking character, were displayed. The various associated bodies and benefit societies exhibited their banners, etc. Salutes in honour of the event were fired at most of the principal cotton and other works. Royal Standards floated from the various churches, the Post Office, stamp office and other public buildings.

Prince Albert, we believe, expressed himself very much pleased with the Dean Mills establishment. His Royal Highness condescended to accept several small samples of cotton in different processes to which it is subjected.

On returning immense multitudes thronged the pathways in the Borough as His Royal Highness went through, the streets presenting to the eye such masses of human beings as never before assembled simultaneously in Bolton. The proceedings were orderly throughout, and the demonstrations of the day must be regarded as a deep manifestation of loyalty."

Whilst the cotton operatives were enjoying the benefits of enforced legislation, other trades and workers were still struggling.

Shop assistants were campaigning for the earlier closure of shops. In November 1852 a public meeting was held in which they stated that their only object was to close their shops at seven o'clock four nights in the week. They complained that nineteen out of every twenty young men employed in drapers' shops were in bad health, for day after day they were confined in the shops and kept there as late as 10 o'clock.

Their campaign met with some success, and this was reported by Mr. Wait, Secretary of the "Early Closing Association", at a meeting in February 1853.

BOLTON CHRONICLE 5th February 1853
"EARLY CLOSING ASSOCIATION –
SOIREE AT THE TEMPERANCE HALL
Mr. Wait, Secretary, read the following report:

The operations of the Society have already been extended to the following trades – drapers, grocers, tea dealers, smallware dealers, haberdashers, etc., the employers of the above trades with very few exceptions, have complied with the requests of the Association to close at 7 p.m. Saturdays and Mondays excepted. This agreement has for the most part been adhered to with a degree of punctuality which is highly creditable; we regret that this cannot be said of all. Most of the employees appear well satisfied with the change, and many have expressed a desire for further abridgement, namely on the evenings of Monday and Saturday. It may not be generally known that great numbers of young men are frequently engaged in shops until 12 o'clock on Saturday evenings, and in some instances as late as one and two o'clock on Sunday mornings. In addition to this great numbers of young persons are employed in millinery, dressmaking, etc., until an equally unreasonable hour.

The resolution was –

'That this meeting desires to record its deep satisfaction at the recent changes of business hours in the drapery and grocery trades of this town, and pledges to assist in carrying out the early closing movement by discountenancing late shopping in their respective families, and inducing others to do the same.' "

The Editorial column in the Bolton Chronicle of 21st May 1853 thought fit to comment on "slavery":

"SLAVERY – AMERICAN AND BRITISH
To admire "Uncle Tom's Cabin" is now highly fashionable, and we are of that fashion, but we must be pardoned if we take leave to express a decided opinion that the fulsome adulation which has been offered to her (Mrs. Harriet Beecher Stowe) since her arrival in the "mother country", is calculated not only to disgust the object of it, but to damage very materially the cause in which she is engaged. Besides it is not very clear that this intense zeal on behalf of slave emancipation is of a very pure and genuine character.

We have had fierce denunciations of slavery from the lips of those who imported thousands of bales of slave-grown cotton. Slavery was horrible, but slave-grown cotton was cheap. They denounced the one and bought the other. It does seem difficult to reconcile a hatred of slavery with an encouragement of slave-grown produce; and they who buy the latter should learn moderation in attacking the former.

But there is another consideration which should curb the tongues of Mrs. Beecher Stowe's adulators in this country. When they are most disposed to inveigh against the slave institutions of America, then should they most carefully consider the condition of their own country. Have we no slavery in England?

An incident has just occurred which is calculated to draw in forcible manner the attention of that lady and the public to a system which too notoriously exists in this boasted land of freedom, which oppresses its victims with a tyranny, in many respects, as bad as that of the American 'domestic institution', and which is hurrying its thousands to an untimely grave.

Mrs. Beecher Stowe, the champion of black slaves of America, was having a dress made in an establishment at the east end of London, in which the young women are kept at work from seven o'clock in the morning until eleven o'clock at night. The whole time allowed these young persons for their meals amounts to 40 minutes each day, thus leaving 15 hours and 20 minutes actual work – that work of the most sedentary and monotonous character imaginable – carried out in a room about 12 feet square, in which a dozen are thus employed from Monday morning until Saturday night. How the Americans will chuckle when they learn that Mrs. Beecher Stowe has been furnished with a dress from such a 'cabin' of white slaves.

It is a national disgrace to us that such a horrible system should be tolerated amongst us. The fault, however, lies more with the public than with proprietors of such establishments. The votaries of fashion are, indeed, the most culpable parties. They have it in their power to put an end to white slavery. They are therefore, chiefly responsible for the guilt of its continuance."

Whilst the Early Closing Association had had limited success with store and shop owners, members of the Borough Council were evidently not co-operative.

BOLTON CHRONICLE *24th May 1856*
"THE MARKET HALL
At a meeting of the Markets Sub-committee on Wednesday last, it was resolved to keep the Market open till nine o'clock each evening during the week, except Saturday, when it will remain open till half-past eleven. This regulation is to remain in force till the end of August."

The Association did, however, announce further success in a notice published in the Bolton Chronicle on 27th September 1856.

"The Committee of the Early Closing Association have great pleasure in announcing to the public that the Drapers, Hosiers, Milliners and Boot and Shoe Dealers, have unanimously agreed to CLOSE THEIR SHOPS, during the winter months at the following hours:–
TUESDAY, WEDNESDAY, THURSDAY AND FRIDAY NIGHTS AT SEVEN
MONDAY AT NINE
SATURDAY AT HALF-PAST TEN.
The public are earnestly desired to support this movement by wholly refraining from LATE SHOPPING."

The success of the curtailment of hours in the cotton trade also led to a universal demand for shorter hours, and a half-day holiday each week.

BOLTON CHRONICLE *24th May 1856*
"THE HALF-DAY HOLIDAY MOVEMENT
On Tuesday last a deputation waited upon the Home Secretary to make a representation on the subject when the Earl of Shaftesbury earnestly pressed upon the attention of Sir George Grey the necessity of 'some relaxation from the pressure of business in these

days of competition and energetic action.'

The only valid, or rather the apparently valid, objection to the scheme is the one urged by Sir George Grey that it would be unreasonable for workmen and others receiving a half holiday on Saturday to expect the same renumeration as though they had worked six full days. Mr. Lilwall disposed of this objection when he said that in all cases where the half-holiday had been granted, and where no deduction had been made in the pay, it was found that the men, exciting themselves with greater spirit, application and energy, really did as much work in the five days and a half, as they did before in six.

This is perfectly consistent with the Ten Hour Act in our mills. We have been assured by several respectable spinners that more work is now being turned out in the various departments of their establishments in ten hours, than could formerly be obtained in twelve hours, and that work is also much better done."

Despite radical pressure the Saturday afternoon holiday enjoyed by the cotton trade was slow to be accepted by other trades.

In spite of improvements in many spheres children were still exploited and used in many trades and occupations. Acts had been in force since the 1780's regulating the use of boys in climbing and sweeping chimneys, and again in 1834, with the introduction of flexible rods and machines, further legislation was enacted to limit the use of 'climbing boys', but there was little enforcement. Under-weight, under-sized boys about eight years old were needed to climb the narrow twisting chimneys – workhouse children were popular choices since they invariably fitted the weight and size requirements – and after a few years' work replacements were needed, for they were soon crippled and useless.

BOLTON CHRONICLE 14th January 1854
"PROHIBITION OF CLIMBING BOYS FOR THE SWEEPING OF CHIMNEYS
At the Borough Court on Saturday last a charge was preferred against Robert Pendlebury, master sweep, of ill-treating William Broadhurst, aged eight years, who was employed by him as a climbing boy. In consequence of complaints which the boy had made of being beaten with a strap, he was taken by a gentleman to the police office yesterday week. He was placed under the care of Mrs. Lomax at the Lock-ups, who stripped and washed him and found several bruises on his shoulders.

The lad, it appeared, had been employed as a climbing boy in

Manchester but the Act which prohibits such employment was there enforced, and in November last he was hired by the defendant for twelve months. Pendlebury paid his parents a pound for his services. It was proved before the Magistrates that the defendant once beat the lad with a strap. Pendlebury stated, in excuse, that the lad had dirty habits.

The Magistrates directed that the lad should be given up to his parents, the defendant to pay expenses, and they intimated that the law prohibiting the employment of climbing boys would, hereafter, be enforced in Bolton.

Pendlebury stated that there were numbers of children not more than five or six years old who followed that occupation."

Chimneys were not the only confined areas requiring boys to clean them –

BOLTON CHRONICLE 20th September 1851
"SHOCKING OCCURRENCE – SUFFOCATION IN A SEWER
Many inhabitants of this town were thrown into a state of excitement on Saturday evening last by reports to the effect that a boy had entered a sewer in Black Horse Street out of which he was unable to return, and that his extraction was likely for being a matter of some difficulty – statements which turned out to be well founded.

The boy who was fourteen years of age, was sent into the sewer owing to its requiring to be cleaned, and he was there confined from about five o'clock on Saturday afternoon, till after eleven in the forenoon of Sunday, when, after various means had been employed to release him from his perilous position, he was taken out dead."

Young children were still employed in coal mines, in worse conditions and in more hazardous occupations than most other industries, and accidents occurred with frequent regularity, and rated only a paragraph in the news.

BOLTON CHRONICLE 20th October 1860
"BOY KILLED AT EDGEFOLD COLLIERY IN WESTHOUGHTON
About ten a.m. on Thursday an accident happened at Edgefold coalmine which occasioned the death of Henry, son of William Crompton of Slack Fold, Little Hulton. The deceased was 10½ years old and employed as a drawer in the pit. He had a strap which was fastened round his back to a tub of coal, which he was guiding down a steep brow. The impetus of the tub overcame his strength,

and he was dragged by it for more than 200 yards, whereby he received mortal injuries and died in about half-an-hour."

The decade had seen a widening of the gulf between the poorer classes. The destitute, the limbless, the sick, the unskilled casual labourer, were still weltering in their hopeless poverty. Pay and conditions in many trades remained pathetic and uncontrolled, but the numerically stronger employees in the cotton trade, and in engineering, augmented by their skill, were beginning to benefit from shorter hours and agreed rates of pay, and were rising in the working class scale to a fairly prosperous position. The low cost of living helped the regular wage earner to enjoy a very tolerable life. Food and drink were cheap. Herrings were sold at three or four for a penny; soles at a penny a pair; cooked meat at 4d a lb; a large loaf for 6d; beer at 1½d a pint; coal at 18s a ton; oranges, pears, grapes plentiful and cheap.

A full range of reigning prices was published in the Bolton Chronicle on 18th January 1851, and in addition to the above, quoted leg of mutton at 6d a lb., sugar at 4d/5½d a lb., bacon at 6½d a lb., and cheese at 7d a lb.

H. Bathe & Co., of No. 8 Deansgate, advertised in the Bolton Chronicle on 8th March 1851, best London Gin at 1s 6d a pint, Jamaica Rum and Scotch Whisky at 2s a pint, and old French Brandy at 3s a pint.

On 30th November 1850, I. Wright of 145 Deansgate advertised "Cheap Winter Clothing";

"Stout Pilot and Whitney overcoats from	12s. 0d.
for boys	8s. 6d.
Fine cloth dress coat	£1. 0s. 0d.
Fancy Cloth Trousers (sic)	10s. 0d.
Mechanics cord or moleskin suits	16s. 6d.

As Christmas approached in 1854 prospective customers were cajoled to buy a variety of good things –

BOLTON CHRONICLE 23rd December 1854
"CHRISTMAS GIFTS
J. TURNBULL, LADIES AND COURT HEAD DRESSER, PERUQUIER AND PERFUMER,
11, New Market, Bolton.
begs to announce to the inhabitants of Bolton and neighbourhood, that he has RE-OPENED his SHOWROOMS for the CHRISTMAS HOLIDAYS, with an extensive and beautiful stock of ENGLISH and FOREIGN FANCY MERCHANDISE, which stands unrivalled for Variety Elegance and Cheapness; and he flatters himself that a visit, which he respectfully solicits, will bear out his assertion. The following are a few of the leading articles of this unique stock:- LADIES AND GENTLEMEN'S DRESSING CASES; COMPANIONS; WRITING DESKS; WORK BOXES; TEA CADDIES; CHINA; BOHEMIAN GLASS ORNAMENTS; ENVELOPE CASES; PORTFOLIOS; BACKGAMMON BOARDS, CHESS AND DRAFT MEN; ACCORDIANS; WAX DOLLS, etc.

A most superb assortment of the most fashionable JEWELLERY, in all branches; French and English PERFUMERY; Sole agents for Titterton's electrifying HAIR BRUSHES; SHELL COMBS IN GREAT VARIETY."

"QUANTITY WITHOUT QUALITY IS WORTH NOTHING ITALIAN HOUSE, 5, CHEAPSIDE, BOLTON.
W. HORSLEY, PROPRIETOR.
BUY your CHRISTMAS PRESENT and NEW YEAR'S GIFTS at the above Establishment.

A splendid and varied Stock, consisting of RICH and BEAUTIFULLY-ORNAMENTED CHRISTMAS CAKES, CHRISTMAS TREES, French and Elva's PLUMS in elegant cartons; Handsome glass and other boxes containing BON-BONS, COSAQUES, CRYSTAL FRUITS, etc., Finest Crown Eleme FIGS, Muscatel RAISINS, Jordan ALMONDS, American APPLES, Jersey PEARS, PINEAPPLES, GRAPES, PUMELLOS, POMEGRANATES, ORANGES, LEMONS, etc., Preserved GINGER, NUTMEGS and ORANGES from China, Crytstallized, Preserved, Dried and Bottled FRUITS from France; Feast's Prize CALF'S FEET JELLY, Nelson's Patent GELATINE; Collin's Prize SARDINES; Keiller's Celebrated MARMALADE, Osborne's Superior ANCHOVY PASTE; POTTED MEATS in great variety; Burgess's much admired PICKLES; and SAUCES; Lebaigue's esteemed CHOCOLATES; CANDIED CITRON, LEMONS AND ORANGES; the finest SPICES, ESSENCES, QUINTESSENCES, etc."

BOLTON CHRONICLE *18th January 1851*
"PRICES OF ARTICLES CONSUMED BY THE
WORKING CLASSES IN 1840 and 1850

	1840	1850
Best Flour per stone	3s. 0d	1s. 0d
Oatmeal	2s. 2d	1s. 8d
Meat – Leg of Mutton per lb	7d	6d
Lard per lb	8d	5½d
Cheese per lb	8d	7d
Bacon per lb	7½d	6½d
Butter – roll of 1½ lb	2s. 0d	1s. 5d
Sugar per lb	7s. 9½d	4s. 5½d
Treacle per lb	4s. 5d	2s. 2½d
Coffee per lb	1s. 6d/2s. 4d	1s. 0d/1s. 8d
Tea per lb	4s. 0d/6s. 0d	3s. 4d/5s. 0d
Soap per lb	5d/6d	4d/5d
Candles per lb	6d	4½d
Rice per lb	2½d/5d	1½d/3½d

The Bolton Chronicle in 1854 reported of "hundreds, if not thousands, of men who earned weekly very high wages. 30s, 40s and, in some cases, 50s was not an uncommon sum."

Certainly a percentage of the working class were no longer struggling for survival, but could enjoy a well fed, well clothed and comfortable life.

HOLIDAYS AND ENTERTAINMENT

The picture of Bolton between those years of 1850 and 1860 has so far been mostly grim and unpleasant, but besides all the filth and misery there was another side to the coin. There were holidays, festive occasions, and regular weekly offerings of entertainment ranging from prim and polite musical evenings to the boisterous, vulgar inhibited concert saloons. Shakespeare and burlesque, melodrama and pantomime, lectures and travelogues, vied with the constant stream of itinerant circuses, diaramas, waxworks, peepshows and fairs.

BOLTON CHRONICLE 4th January 1851
"CHRISTMAS AND NEW YEAR
Throughout Christendom 'Christmas' is celebrated immediately it arrives, and the New Year no sooner dawns than it receives its homage. An exception to the rule, however, obtained in Bolton till within the last few years, which still partially remains. Not long ago the natal day of the Redeemer was pretty generally disregarded in this town, and a holiday was generally observed on New Years day. Now, though a holiday takes place on Christmas day, the beginning of the New Year is looked upon as *the* Christmas season, and the inhabitants betake themselves to their festivities accordingly. Christmas geese, pies, puddings and beer don't see the light until New Year's eve, and Christmas weddings and parties are deferred till the following day.

This was the order of things in regard to the past festive season. Christmas day having passed with its cessation from labour and its appointed ordinances, New Year's eve overtook us on Tuesday at the close of which day the mills, foundries, bleaching establishments, etc., etc. were closed, some for the day, others for two, and the work people retired to their homes in anticipation of an annual treat.

The termination at midnight of 1850 was speedily followed by the ringing of bells of the Parish Church and for hours before the break of day sounds of music were plentifully poured forth in the streets by companies of vocalists and instrumentalists, indicative of the compliments of the season. The fall of a considerable quantity of rain seemed not to damp the ardour of persons going about to wish their friends a happy New Year.

The weather at this festive time was quite of an unusual character, frost and snow being out of the question, and the atmosphere exceedingly mild. On New Years Day from nine o'clock till four, little, if any, rain descended. The town rapidly became a scene of life and bustle, and so it continued until evening approached. Boys and girls, young men and maids, fathers and mothers, thronged the streets in quest of pleasure. The "festive array" in which many of the Boltonians and their visitors were clad bore ample testimony to the existence of that 'prosperity' which everyone desired to reign throughout the year, and the very 'respectable' nature of the apparel displayed on the backs of the working classes strikingly illustrated the cheapness and plentitude of articles of dress. Candidates for married bliss were moderately prominent in processions, wending their way amidst the 'busy hum of men'. Bands of music passed stylishly through the borough, and added an air of 'harmony' to that of goodwill. The multitudes of country people who flocked to the town in the early part of the day increased the population vastly above its ordinary amount, and the 'fair' was attended most numerously.

The principal streets were crowded to an extent which was rarely, if ever, exceeded. The shops were set out to the best advantage. Stalls with oranges, nuts, gingerbread and other eatable nicnacs (sic), which it would be wearisome to enumerate, were abundant, and there was no lack of toys either in regard to quantity or variety. On the market-place holiday amusements in the shape of swinging-boats, whirligigs, etc., were in active operation, and there was an abundance of shows and showmen, professing to enlighten, inform, or amuse on subjects natural and unnatural, historical and dramatical, artistical, mystical, gymnastical. On no former occasion in our remembrance has the market place been so densely crowded as it was on Wednesday by pleasure seekers, money seekers and their appliances. Not the least remarkable sight in the town generally was the great number of those who had imbibed to an immoderate extent the infusions of malt and other potent beverages. In the evening Sunday School and Congregational tea parties were held in different parts of the town, and other means of recreation were resorted to."

Thus was Christmas and New Year celebrated, and Easter was the next holiday to anticipate.

Holidays and Entertainment

BOLTON CHRONICLE 2nd April 1852
"EASTER FAIR
A fair is always held in Bolton on Easter Monday. The "business of the day" consists chiefly of visits by country folk to the town, the perambulating of the principal thoroughfares to see, and be seen, and enjoying whatever pleasures Bolton can provide in the shape of travelling exhibitions, refreshments – indoor and out – or any pastime concomitants which may present themselves; many of the factories and workshops being also closed in the afternoon, in order that their occupants may join in the recreations. From these combined causes the town is usually as thronged over Easter Monday as on any day in the year, and this time was no exception to the rule.

Monday last was highly favourable to the pursuits common to the season, the weather being dry, bracing and pleasant. The sources of gratification for the holiday folk did not appear as plentiful as they have sometimes been. The most remarkable deficiency was in the exhibitions of which there was a meagre display, three or four not quite first class shows forming the complement of that class of entertainment. The shows occupied a portion of the ground usually set aside to such purposes on the Market Place, and the square was crowded with stalls, ordinary and extraordinary; children's swings in varied form and appearance; human beings of all ages and sizes; and an abundance of life everywhere streaming forth in pushings, jostlings, juvenile exultations, and an indescribable medley of noises, not the least noticeable of which were the earthly and unearthly dins emanating from the musical (?) performers connected with caravans, etc. Deansgate, Bradshawgate, Market Street and other streets were thronged during the day, and everywhere there seemed to be as much joyousness as ever for Easter Fair. The annual show of entire horses took place at the Cattle Market in the afternoon, and interested many hundreds of town and country people. Eight or nine animals were displayed, including fine specimens of thoroughbred coach and cart horses."

Eastertime festivities did, however, on occasion present problems. Eastertime was also an Egg Feast, symbolic of the beginning of Spring. Pagan rites had become inter-related with the Christian festival of the Resurrection, and Lancashire tradition had produced "Pace-Egging" – a ritual of dressing-up and wandering the streets in gangs begging for eggs. These gangs of men and youths, and sometimes women, adorned themselves with ribbons and coloured paper, blacked their faces, and armed themselves with wooden swords and staves, as well as baskets for collecting the eggs in. When rival groups met fights were not improbable. The activities of the "Pace-Eggers" brought comment from the Bolton Chronicle, and appearances at the Borough Court.

BOLTON CHRONICLE 10th April 1852
"PACE EGGING
During the past week the practice of pace egging has been revived in Bolton, as is usual at this season, and no small number of persons have availed themselves of the opportunity thus afforded of earning for themselves a very great amount of disgrace, and at the same time afflicting upon the decenter portion of society much annoyance. We are sorry to state that some of the disgusting features of the custom have been exhibited by females, who seemed to glory in them."

BOLTON CHRONICLE 17th April 1852
"PACE EGGING
The subject of pace egging was brought before the Mayor, and J. Arrowsmith, Esq., at the Borough Court on Saturday last in one of its more offensive forms, by the investigation of charges of disorderly conduct preferred against three young men.

From the evidence adduced it appeared that on the Thursday night previous a disturbance was created at the Old Millstone public house, Deansgate, which resulted in the destruction of a number of pots and other materials, and the infliction of sundry violent blows upon persons happening to be present. Two or three police officers who had been sent for to restore order being amongst the parties assaulted, as was also Mrs. McKay, the wife of the Landlord. Two parties of Pace eggers had come in contact at the Millstone, and begun fighting, which was carried on with large, heavy sticks, in a company of sixty or seventy persons. The principal actors in the affair had their faces blackened, so that detection of the features was difficult.

The Mayor said that the case was a serious one and conduct such as the accused had been engaged in could not be allowed in this town.

Two fined 20s or be imprisoned for twenty one days, the other fined 5s and costs, or seven days."

The next holiday – Whitsun – soon followed upon the Easter festivities:

BOLTON CHRONICLE 14th June 1851
"WHITSUNTIDE AT BOLTON
The Whitsun holidays in this town are this year, as usual being observed at the end of Whitsun Week, instead of the beginning as

in many other places, but the rule has slightly been departed from on account of the attractions of the Great Exhibition at Hyde Park, a few Boltonians having left their homes on Saturday, Monday and other days, for London. General cessation from work at the mills and other large establishments commenced on Thursday evening and will continue till Monday, and, to all appearances, the people are bent upon enjoying themselves heartily.

The weather up to Thursday was not for the most part propitious to pleasure seekers and gloomy indications doubtless depressed the spirits of hundreds who built upon entering upon the holiday time with joyous feelings. Appearances were not very promising at an early hour on Friday morning as regarded the portentions of the sky, yet the "cock's shrill clarion" had not long been heard before the streets were scenes of bustle created by the stirring folks desirous of availing themselves of the means of enjoyment now greatly in favour – that of travelling by excursion trains to the port of Liverpool, or some other watering place, or town in the country. As the day advanced and locomotives whizzed along the railways with huge loads of passengers the signs of the weather became hopeful, and notwithstanding the absence of parasols and the abundance of umbrellas evinced extensive preparations for a rainy day, the day was fair and agreeable to those who remained in Bolton and its vicinity.

A prominent feature of Whit Friday in the Borough was the great proportion of closed shops. This feature is more remarkable every year, and if we go on as hitherto the holiday will ere long be something like universal. Many of the occupants of the shops had no doubt gone off either by rail or some other mode of conveyance and in one way or another the population of the town was very largely reduced for twelve or fifteen hours. On no similar occasion for many years has there been such dullness in regard to festive scenes. School processions have almost, like the club demonstrations of former years, disappeared; not a note of music was to be heard in the streets from any of the local bands; and fewer social gatherings were got up than usual. There must have been a falling off too in 'Whitsun ale', though here and there certain personages could hardly maintain a tolerable equilibrium.

In the latter portion of the day, nevertheless, hundreds of decently clad people, with pleasant countenance and easy air, perambulated the principal streets, which were profusely laid out with stalls of oranges and sundry tempting comestibles, the Market Place also containing a number of ordinary contrivances for amusing the young. The evening was not only the throngest part of the day in the town, but the most agreeable; it was clear, bright and sweet. We find from inquiry at the railway station that the following number of passengers left Bolton yesterday by cheap

trains:
      2,400 to Southport
      1,560 to Blackpool
and   500 to Lytham.
About 400 booked for the Isle of Man; 3,773 left in the course of the day for the Manchester Races.

At the Great Moor Street Station 1,297 excursionists started for Liverpool."

BOLTON CHRONICLE 31st May 1851
"LONDON AND NORTH-WESTERN RAILWAY
BOLTON AND KENYON LINE
WHIT-WEEK EXCURSION TRAINS FROM BOLTON
TO LIVERPOOL AND BACK
Excursion trains consisting of First, Second and Third class carriages will leave the Railway Station, Great Moor Street, for Lime Street Station, Liverpool on
THURSDAY, FRIDAY AND SATURDAY, 12th, 13th and 14th June,
at 7 o'clock in the morning and will return from Liverpool to Bolton on each of the above days at half-past seven o'clock in the evening.
Fares from Bolton to Liverpool and back
First Class   5s.
Second Class   3s. 9d.
Third Class (covered carriages)   2s. 6d."

Entertainment and enlightenment was not only proffered on festive occasions, but throughout the year there was a variety of diversiments providing you had the energy and the money to attend.

Temperance Halls, Concert Rooms and Halls advertised their attractions.

BOLTON CHRONICLE 11th August 1850
ADVERTISEMENT
"CROWDED ATTENDANCE
THE ANATOMICAL VENUS
IMPARTING USEFUL INFORMATION TO EVERY INDIVIDUAL
THE VENUS TAKES TO PIECES FROM HEAD TO FOOT AND FROM THE OUTER SKIN TO THE BONES, SHOWING THE ENTIRE STRUCTURE OF THE HUMAN BODY.
THOSE DESIROUS OF GAINING IMPORTANT

KNOWLEDGE MUST MAKE AN EARLY CALL, AS THE EXHIBITION WILL SHORTLY CLOSE.
Open from TEN to FOUR –   One Shilling
 and from
         SIX to NINE –   Sixpence
           A LECTURE EVERY HOUR
LADIES ADMITTED ON MONDAYS AND FRIDAYS
ABOUT 200 LADIES VISITED THE EXHIBITION THIS WEEK.
———— TEMPERANCE HALL ————"

BOLTON CHRONICLE 30th November 1850
ADVERTISEMENT
"STAR CONCERT ROOM AND MUSEUM
COME TO THE "STAR" AND LET NOT THE GOLDEN OPPORTUNITY PASS OF GAINING A FREE TICKET FOR THE EXHIBITION OF 1851.
COME AND SEE THE WONDROUS REDMAN OR DISLOCATED MORTAL.
LAUGH TILL YOUR SIDES ACHE AT THE SONGS, DUETS AND RECITATIONS OF MR & MRS MUNRO.
SHRIEK WITH MERRIMENT AT THE WHIMSICALITIES OF THE BROTHERS KENNEDY.
PONDER WITH PLEASURE UPON THE DELIGHTFUL BALLAD SINGING OF MRS. FOXCROFT
and
MARVEL AT THAT MIRACLE OF LITERATURE, CHARLES SLOMAN, WHO DELIVERS POEMS UPON THE INSTANT ON SUBJECTS PROPOSED BY THE AUDIENCE."

The "Star" Concert Room was one of the forms of entertainment which a number of Boltonians wished to see closed. They offended by their incitment to intemperance and their bawdiness. With this aim in view the inevitable 'public meeting' was held.

BOLTON CHRONICLE 21st August 1852
"PUBLIC MEETINGS ON SINGING SALOONS
A public meeting was held on Thursday evening last to take into consideration the best means to adopt for counteracting the evil tendencies of Singing Saloons, Beerhouses, etc.
The Rev. B. C. Etheridge addressed the meeting –
It has long been my earnest desire to see the Christian public of Bolton aroused to some united effort to counteract the baneful influence of these places of entertainment.

It may perhaps be thought very strange, but I am not ashamed to confess that I have visited one of the most notorious of these places, one which happily now does not exist. It has long been my custom to warn the young people of my congregation and Sabbath School against attending that place in particular, and that I might not overstate its demoralising influence, nor speak without that awareness so important a caution demanded, I attended part of an evening's entertainment, and although I had formed a very low opinion from what I had heard of the place, I found when I stood in that gallery and gazed down upon the scene no language would be too strong to deprecate the whole affair.

Rather than being in what had been termed by some a place of amusement, I felt I was in the suburbs of hell. It was an ordinary occasion, but I should think there were at least a thousand persons present most of whom were from twelve to twenty-four years of age. The place was so crowded that the waiters were unable to walk upon the floor and were therefore hopping about among the heads of the people on the backs of the seats, handing them pipes of tobacco and various kinds of drink and spiritous liquors. Young people of both sexes were huddled together into the closest contact, and most of them appeared to be freely using the spiritous provisions of the bar. In the midst of this uproar a tall well dressed female came on to the platform and attracted their attention by a song. I do not say that the song was immoral, but I do affirm that the gestures of the lady who sang it, together with the stimulating influence of the drink, and the whole scene, were calculated to excite the basest passions of the human mind.

Resolution – That a united effort on the part of Christian ministers, Sabbath School teachers, parents and other friends of religious education is necessary, and recommend, as a preliminary step, the presentation of a memorial to the Borough Magistrates, on or before the 26th inst., that being the annual licensing day."

The following week's edition of the Bolton Chronicle brought forth comments from Boltonians in letters to the Editor, one of which read –

"Sir,
Again most of the cases mentioned might have been avoided if these who now pretend to take such an interest in the welfare of the masses had come forward and provided rational amusements and healthy sports for the young; but unfortunately those who are now endeavouring to put down singing saloons, are those who would put down all kinds of amusements, and make all as pharisaical as themselves. Provide a substitute at low charges, let it be interesting and amusing, we shall then cease to complain of singing saloons

robbing our Sunday schools. What do these philanthropic individuals offer now to the young? Nothing, unless we reckon sermons and railway trips."

The Annual Licensing Meeting was duly held on 26th August 1852.

BOLTON CHRONICLE 28th August 1852
"*ANNUAL LICENSING MEETING*
Prior to the hearing of applicants for new spirit licences, a deputation from the public meeting of Thursday evening week came into Court to present a memorial on the subject of singing saloons. Mr. Winder inquired if the deputation were prepared with any plan to suppress the evil complained of. Mr. Heaton said they had merely to recommend the Magistrates to apply the law with the utmost stringency to compel the occupiers of singing saloons to keep their establishments in order, as intemperance and other irregularities were practised in them.

Mr. Cullen remarked that he believed the police would have instructions to look into the matters in question and the magistrates would do everything they could to suppress the evils complained of."

The notorious place that Rev. Etheridge referred to as "one which happily now does not exist", was the Star Concert Room and Museum, which was destroyed by fire on 13th July 1852 – an event which was reported at considerable length by the Chronicle:

BOLTON CHRONICLE 17th July 1852
"*DESTRUCTION OF THE STAR CONCERT ROOM BY FIRE*
The building known as the Star Concert Room and Museum was destroyed in the course of Tuesday night, when it became the scene of one of the most alarming fires that have taken place in this Borough for some years.

The Star Concert Room and Museum, as our readers are aware, has, for a considerable period, formed a point of attraction to thousands of the inhabitants of Bolton and the neighbourhood, who have resorted thither more or less frequently for the purpose of amusement or recreation, entertainments having been provided ever-varying and of a character which always drew interested or admiring audiences; and the destruction of the premises by fire will be remembered perhaps equally in consequence of the amount of property devoured, and the fact of that property embracing a very notable establishment.

The building was erected a little more than twelve years ago by Mr. Thomas Sharples, then of the Millstone Tavern, Crown Street, who subsequently occupied it in connection with the Star Inn, a public house in Churchgate previously called the Cock Inn. It stood immediately behind the "Star", and was in three general divisions or storeys, the first on the ground floor, used for the purposes of a brewhouse, stable, yard, paint shop, workshops, etc., the second the concert room, and the third the museum. Above the museum was a promenade, forming in great measure the roof of the building; the south end being distinguished by the mast of a large ship, with a quantity of rigging.

The great object of attraction was the concert room – an apartment extending the whole length and breadth of the building, with galleries at the side and north end, and a theatre stage at the south end. The concert room was laid out with seats and drinking tables, and under the end gallery was a bar from which ale, spirits, and refreshments were retailed to visitors. The entertainments provided in this part of the establishment were on the weekday evenings, Monday afternoons, and at pastimes during the whole day, and comprised music, comic and sentimental singing, living tableaux, etc. etc. The museum extended over the concert room, from which it was approached by a long flight of stairs. Many objects of a rare and curious character were displayed in the museum, which was open to inspection at all hours of the day. Amongst the collection was a number of wax figures, models, sundry views, pictures, stuffed reptiles and birds, geological specimens, busts, moving mechanical figures, living monkeys, etc.

In the museum also, on the right of the entrance, was fitted up Mr. J. Benfold's "temple of magic". Mr. Benfold kept on hand, as the catalogue stated, apparatus for playing deceptive, but pleasing, experiments, the use of which might be taught to such as would become purchasers. The same gentleman had also rooms on the promenade for taking photographic portraits.

The promenade, which was considerably narrower than the concert room, owing to the slanting roof on each side of the museum, was floored with timber, laid upon lead, with fence railings at the ends and sides, and on fine days people would often spend an hour or two in viewing thence the town and country. An artificial pond, formed of an iron cistern, was placed at the north end, behind which were two prominent objects in the shape of representations of a Cherokee Indian and a colossal female figure from a ship named "Phoebus".

Here then was a large building in flames in the midst of a spot thickly studded with cottages, shops, inns, and other erections, embracing all the property within the south side of Churchgate, the east side of Bradshawgate, Princes Street, and the north end of School Street. Though Churchgate is one of the most favourable parts of the town for the application of the Corporation valves, as a good pressure of water extends thither, comparatively little was done in this respect for saving property, till the most important part of the mischief by the fire had actually taken place.

The raging of the flames, combined with numerous and vivid flashes of lightning, had an awful effect. The fire quickly spread itself over the entire building, and at length formed an enormous blaze rising into the air.

The mast and rigging blazed with conspicuousness for some time, till at length the former fell with a crash upon a cottage in Glaizebrook Lane, and forced in a portion of the roof.

The scene was rendered more dismal by the occupants of the cottages in Wigan Lane, Oliver Lane and Glaizebrook Lane, removing their scanty furniture from their humble and unsafe abodes into the streets, a course the adoption of which, more or less, was also deemed advisable by Mr. Charnley, butcher, Mr. Harwood, gingerbeer manufacturer, Mr. Thompson of the Angel public house, Miss Norris, confectioner, Bradshawgate, Mr. Crompton, gilder, Bradshawgate, and others. With respect to the damage done by fire, we believe it will probably amount to £6,000 or £7,000. It has been said that considerable time elapsed between the giving of the alarm and any effective force of water being applied for extinguishing the fire, which, as already intimated, is true. Another complaint refers to the want of order amongst the firemen, and to general confusion amongst those who worked and managed the engines, some of whom would make a great noise, and curse and swear in the discharge of their duties. This can scarcely be a matter of surprise when the Superintendent of the fire brigade was drunk, and it may be of satisfaction to the public to know that he was discharged by the Fire and Police Committee on Wednesday."

This matter of drunkenness among Bolton's population was a regular matter of concern to the advocates of temperance.

BOLTON CHRONICLE 12th February 1853
"*MISSION TO DRUNKARDS*
The fact is becoming more apparent every day that drunkenness is pre-eminently the sin of Great Britain, and that drunkards are lowest in the scale of civilization and morals. They are in reality the 'heathen at home'. They are the blight and pestilence of the family circle, the employer's vexation, the public burden, a dishonour to the human form, and the reproach and scandal of a professed Christian country. They are the centres of the worst forms of wretchedness and cruelty.

At the earnest solicitation of a number of gentlemen, the Committee of the Bolton Temperance Society have resolved, in order to give additional efficiency to their ordinary efforts on behalf of this unfortunate class, to employ a Temperance Missionary, and for that important work they have selected Mr. W. Gregson. His mission is to the drunkards of Bolton. He will visit them at their homes, and when reason and reflection are not silenced by the intoxicating agent, converse with them about a 'more excellent way'.

As its successful carrying out will involve additional expenditure donations and subscriptions will be thankfully received."

There is no record of the success or otherwise of this missionary work, but in 1854 there was a meeting held in the Temperance Hall for the inauguration of the Bolton Auxiliary of the United Kingdom Alliance for the Legal Suppression of the Liquor Traffic. The object of the United Kingdom Alliance was to obtain a legislative enactment totally and entirely prohibiting the sale of intoxicating liquor.

Another popular place of entertainment was the Theatre Royal in Churchgate, and the proprietor had hopes of attracting the large numbers who had patronised the Star Concert Hall, by staging the "Star" type of entertainment, but without the availability of beer and spirits.

BOLTON CHRONICLE 26th March 1853
ADVERTISEMENT
"THEATRE ROYAL, CHURCHGATE, BOLTON
A rumour having been widely circulated that the Bolton Theatre was being metamorphosed into a singing saloon with a beer licence, and such report being not only incorrect, but injurious, the Proprietor takes this opportunity to inform all who desire to know his future intentions in the management of the above old established place of amusement.

THE DRAMA
is evidently popular only with a few, having failed to be as remunerative to the most worthy managers as other amusements.

CONCERT ROOMS
are objected to by a most influential class, through their alleged tendency to encourage drinking, which, though a mistaken idea, has taken deep root, and as the old saying goes 'give a dog a bad name and hang it'.

The Theatrical Season having expired gives an opportunity to try and experiment in testing whether the same style that proved popular so many years to the working classes at

THE STAR INN

Will be received by them without being associated with drink, and in trying this experiment W.S. hopes to have the good wishes and assistance of all who desire the experiment to succeed, and respectfully solicits the countenance of the authorities, that he may maintain order, without which nothing can prosper.

On MONDAY next, being EASTER MONDAY, the amusements will commence at ONE O'CLOCK, TWO O'CLOCK, THREE O'CLOCK AND EVERY HOUR TILL TEN AT NIGHT, and at HALF PAST SEVEN O'CLOCK EVERY OTHER EVENING DURING THE WEEK.

Promenade 3d.   Gallery 2d.

THE SIX BLACK DWARFS
AS THE ORLEANS SERENADERS

will be found particularly amusing, the bone castinets, banjo, tambourine, violin, etc., being handled so humorously by these little creatures, averaging only two feet six inches in height, and ranging from 10 to 20 years old, and so clever an imitation that if not known must be taken for living beings.

THE GRAND DIORAMA OF THE SHIP ON FIRE

It is so marvellously exciting and interesting.

Splendid Dioramic picture of an OLD ENGLISH CHURCH, EXPRESS TRAIN BY NIGHT, etc. etc.

THE COMBAT BETWEEN THE WILD HORSE AND LION,
etc.
MUSICAL ACCOMPANIMENTS

W.S. has also very great pleasure in further announcing that other arrangements are pending which will greatly increase the amusements and diversify the entertainments, due notice of which will be given, the whole forming a brief but brilliant entrement."

Varied entertainment continued to be provided at the Theatre Royal, but probably with limited success, in view of the lack of bar facilities.

Drama was back on stage for the winter season, and the following advert appeared on the 4th September 1858:

"THEATRE ROYAL, CHURCHGATE

will open this evening for the Winter Season.

NEW COMPANY
On this evening, Saturday, 4th September the performance will commence with Buckstone's drama of:
THE WRECKERS or a MARINER'S DREAM
to conclude with the melodrama of
THE WOOD DEMON

MONDAY	— day performance at half-past two o'clock THE HUNCH BACK
TUESDAY	— THE RACE OF LIFE or RAKE'S PROGRESS
WEDNESDAY	— THE BEAR HUNTERS
FRIDAY	— First Fashionable Night THE SCHOOL FOR SCANDAL
Admission:	— Centre Box 1s. Side Boxes and Pit 6d. Gallery 3d.

The Rule for EXPELLING those parties guilty of SMOKING will be rigorously enforced."

There was too entertainment of a higher cultural level, and in 1859 a new Concert Hall was opened in Mawdsley Street.

BOLTON CHRONICLE 10th February 1859
"OPENING OF NEW CONCERT HALL
The new Concert Hall in Mawdsley Street was worthily inaugurated on Tuesday evening, with Mr. Charles Hallé's third subscription concert. The spacious hall has a light and very elegant appearance, and a more brilliant assemblage has never before been witnessed in this town than was congregated within its walls on its opening night. Altogether there would be about nine hundred persons present and the general feeling was one of hearty satisfaction with the appearance of the place. The orchestra, as usual, in Mr. Hallé's concerts, was a most efficient one, including some of the leading instrumentalists in the country."

Two names famous in the world of entertainment appeared in Bolton – the celebrated Christy's Minstrels gave two performances at the Concert Hall on Tuesday and Wednesday 25th and 26th October 1859, and an advertisement in the Bolton Chronicle on 23rd October 1858 announced:

"GENERAL TOM THUMB
Under the special patronage of the Queen and the principal crowned Heads of Europe.
The original and celebrated American General TOM THUMB

who had the honour of appearing three times before Her Majesty and the Royal Family in the year 1844, will give his farewell entertainments at the
TEMPERANCE HALL
on Monday and Tuesday, November 1st and 2nd 1858.

The little General will ride to and from the Temperance Hall in his miniature chariot, drawn by the smallest ponies in the world, attended by an African coachman and footmen in livery.

Two exhibitions on Monday, November 1st from Three to half-past Four o'clock and from half-past seven o'clock to Nine o'clock.

Three exhibitions on Tuesday, from Twelve to half-past one, from three to half-past four, and from half-past seven to nine o'clock.

Doors open half-an-hour in advance.

Admission – Day exhibitions 1s. Children under 10 6d.

Evening Exhibitions for the accommodation of all classes the admission will be 6d, regardless of age.

Reserved seats 1s."

The singing saloons were not the only places regarded as dens of iniquity. A section of the Bolton community regarded anything connected with the theatrical profession as immoral.

Members of the Bolton Cricket Club endeavoured to raise funds for the Bolton Infirmary and Dispensary by staging a concert at the Theatre Royal, a laudable object which was not appreciated by some Boltonians, one of whom wrote to the Editor of the Bolton Chronicle a letter dated 27th September 1851 –

"To the Editor of the Bolton Chronicle.
Sir,
BOLTON CRICKET CLUB AND THE PLAYHOUSE
Your paper of Saturday last announced a performance to take place on the 26th inst., in aid of the funds of the Bolton Infirmary and Dispensary. Will you permit me to express my dissent to this questionable mode of raising a few pounds, and to suggest to the Vicar of Bolton, and the Gentlemen of the Dispensary Committee, that their influence for good would be much better exerted by checking these young aspirants in their soaring propensities for histrionic fame.

I, for one, doubt the propriety of the "exhibition" altogether, yet if the funds of the institution required such unusual assistance, surely a more elegant selection of pieces might have been made – a couple of lower, coarser, more stupid, morbid and nonsensical pieces of trash could not have been fixed upon than those advertised; they are unfit for the ears of ladies, and unbecoming the tastes of gentlemen; and except that they afforded an opportunity for the exposure of childish vanity and ridiculous parade, I know no earthly object to be gained by this occasional display.

If a real desire to excel in dramatic literature inspired these cricket gents, they might assemble in the Mechanics Institution or some suitable other place, for the study of elocution, and thus exercise and give tone to their delicate minds, to the neglect of the getting up of 'extravaganza shows', such as "Fortunes Frolic", "Bombastes Furioze", "Black Eyed Susan" and (least and I hope the last) "Tom Thumb".

It is astonishing Mr. Editor, how low great minds may descend. It is the fault of sensible persons how far they descend with them.

Let the 'guardians' of these amateurs whose labours are self-imposed, take care of them; and let all who patronise these pantomimists remember, that to encourage such farcical exhibitions is unsafe to the morals of the striplings engaged, whatever mock charity may be pleaded for the object of the institution.

Yours truly,
    A PARENT."

The Bolton Chronicle's review of the night's entertainment read:

"The amateur performance by members of the Bolton Cricket Club in aid of the funds of the Bolton Infirmary, took place last night in the presence of a moderately numerous auditory, including the Mayor, ex-Mayor, a number of the Infirmary Committee, and many respectable and influential inhabitants of the Borough.

The pieces selected for the occasion were "Black Eyed Susan" and "Tom Thumb", in the former of which the efforts of the cricketers were not productive of so much effect as might have been desired. This is naturally attributed to the drama being, to a considerable extent, unfitted to any but professional actors. "Tom Thumb" was attended with better success, the music being given in a creditable manner, and some of the characters very well sustained."

Another cry to Authority to put a halt to wicked pastimes was made on 21st February 1852 –

Letter to the Editor, Bolton Chronicle
"Sir,
Pigeon Flying
I hope you will find room in your paper to acquaint the authorities of Bolton, Farnworth and neighbourhood, that pigeon flying is carried on to a great extent on the Sabbath day. The practice is for young men and lads from 14 to 20 years of age, to bring pigeons to Bolton on a Sunday and fly them to Farnworth for wagers. The extent of such an evil you can scarcely imagine, the parties who practise such conduct are guilty also of drinking and all manner of gaming.

There is one practice connected with this pigeon flying which I think may be easily put a stop to, and to which I would call the attention of the railway companies. I allude to railway guards taking pigeons from different parts of the country to Liverpool, Fleetwood and other places for the purpose of putting them up.

No wonder that our Sunday Schools are not better attended, and that the morals of the working classes are not of a higher standard whilst such Sabbath desecration is permitted.

Yours truly."

It is not surprising that emphasis was put on providing entertainment for the 'working classes', when you take into account that out of a population of nearly 115,000 only just over 2,500 were males owning property with a rateable value in excess of £10. Advertised entertainment to attract the 'gentry' rarely appeared in the columns of the Bolton Chronicle, but two such adverts did appear in December 1854 –

BOLTON CHRONICLE December 1854
"FOURTH ANNUAL GRAND MASONIC BALL (to which non-Masons will be admitted) will be held in the Bath's Assembly Rooms on 6th December in aid of the Patriotic Fund.
Tickets (including refreshments) admitting a Lady and a Gentleman, One Guinea
Ladies single Tickets – 7s. 6d.
Masonic Brethren are requested to appear in the full dress clothing of their Rank and office.
Kohler's Band will be in attendance.
Dancing to commence at 9 p.m."

GRAND ORATORIO
  MENDELSSOHN'S SACRED ORATORIO
    OF
      "ELIJAH"

will be performed in the Temperance Hall on Wednesday evening, the 13th December.
Principals – Miss Birch, Miss Lascelles
          Mr. Alfred Pierre and
          Mr. F. H. Bodda
            (of the London Concerts)
Tickets – Reserved seats 5s. Gallery 3s.
          Promenade 1s. 6d."

The biggest event of the decade was, without doubt, the Great Exhibition of 1851. Inspired by Prince Albert, the idea of the exhibition was gradually accepted by the majority. The minority forecast every conceivable disastrous result; fear of an unruly working class, an invasion of Papists, and the establishment of brothels. Colonel Sibthorp, M.P., one of the more eloquent objectors, said though he did not wish to see the building destroyed by any acts of violence, he would to God that some hailstorm, or some visitation of lightning, might descend to defeat the ill-advised project.

Joseph Paxton designed the unique iron and glass exhibition hall, well named the "Crystal Palace", and with incredible speed the building was completed in seven months.

By the beginning of 1850 the "Exhibition" had created universal interest. On 10th February 1850 the Editorial column in the Bolton Chronicle declared:

"The purpose of the Great Exhibition of the Works of Industry of All Nations, for the original idea of the which we are indebted to His Royal Highness, Prince Albert, is, as a contemporary has fairly described it, to bring together in one comprehensive gathering the productions of every people in the world, so that artists, manufacturers, and mechanics of this country will be enabled to compare the results of their skill with those produced by the ingenuity and industry of fellow-workmen in other lands, see wherein they excel or are deficient; what wants are unsupplied, where they may dread or defy comparison; how they may be benefited by the adoption and extension of others' inventions or improvements; what fields of art and industry remain but partly occupied; and wherein they may most advance by persevering most.

There will be four grand divisions. First, the raw material, second the machinery and mechanical inventions by which the material is turned into useful or ornamental shape. Third, the manufactures produced by such machinery, and fourth, the triumphs of sculpture and plastic art generally."

By August interest had been further aroused and the following notice appeared in the Bolton Chronicle on 17th August 1850:

"GREAT EXHIBITION OF THE WORKS OF INDUSTRY
OF ALL NATIONS
THE BOLTON LOCAL COMMITTEE TO BOLTON WORKMEN

It is almost certain that every intelligent Mechanic and Artisan who is anxious to improve himself in his particular trade, and thereby advance his position in society, will not fail to visit London in the course of the summer or autumn of 1851, to examine the Industrial Works of all Nations, which will then be exhibited.

Because, at a trifling expense of time and money, he may leisurely examine the raw materials and manufactured products of the whole globe, which hitherto the very wealthy only have been able to see, and that by an immense expenditure in travelling.

Because he can, with agreeable companions of his own choice, see the great Metropolis of his country, of which every Englishman may be reasonably proud, and enjoy an outing which, if arranged with reasonable care, must result in pleasure and profit.

The expense of the journey would probably be:

For railway fare to London and back	£1. 0s. 0d.
8 breakfasts at 9d., 8 dinners at 1s., 8 suppers at 9d.–	£1. 0s. 0d.
6 beds at 1s. 2d. and malt liquor or tea 1s. a day	16s. 0d.
Fees of admission to various exhibitions, with expense of a trip by steamer up and down the Thames	£1. 0s. 0d.
Extras	4s. 0d.
TOTAL	£4. 0s. 0d.

For these exhibitions and excursions it is calculated that 45 hours will be required, which leaves about 30 hours to see free exhibitions, public buildings, streets, parks, churches, etc.

Thus it appears that for a working-man's visit to London eight days time and four pounds in money are required. No doubt the visit may be made for less money in less time, but not with such a share of comfort and such opportunity to examine the objects of curiosity with attention as is here suggested.

No extra expense for clothing is recommended. At this Exhibition a cleanly, decent working man will be respected in his own character.

To save £4 from the wages of a year 1s. 6½d. must be set aside for

52 weeks, but to allow for accident it is recommended that 1s. 9d. per week be the sum saved, commencing on the first Saturday of September.

It is recommended that workmen immediately commence their arrangements by associating themselves into convenient parties, not exceeding 20, if possible, of the same trade, and nearly the same age and of congenial habits, tastes and opinions in religion and politics. To appoint one of their number, in whom all have confidence, to receive their weekly contributions, which should be regularly deposited in the Savings Bank."

The Bolton Chronicle was critical of the absence of cotton yarn from Bolton spinners:

BOLTON CHRONICLE 17th May 1851
"BOLTON CONTRIBUTIONS TO THE GREAT EXHIBITION
It must be confessed that the display made by the Bolton Cotton Manufacturers, though very excellent as far as it goes, is nevertheless deficient in many important particulars. Thus, there is no exhibitor of cotton yarns, though many thousands of our population occupy their lives in the production of this article, but one firm which had been at great expense and trouble in preparing samples of yarns (among which was some of extreme fineness) by an unhappy accident had the whole destroyed by fire, together with the case in which they were to have been exhibited, the very day on which they were completed and ready for transmission to London."

The firm referred to was T & J Heaton, Delph Hill Mill (Doffcocker), later at Lostock Junction Mills, who had spun an incredible 800's cotton count specially for the Exhibition. The spinning was repeated, but too late for the Exhibition, and the intention was to present the yarn and display case to Prince Albert on his visit to Bolton. Story has it that this was done, and that the case was on display at Osborne House. Enquiries with the Curator at Osborne House have failed to substantiate this story. Samples of the yarn were, however, on show in the offices of William Heaton & Sons, at Lostock, and the writer has a small sample of this yarn.

A club was formed in Bolton to encourage and organise trips to the Exhibition –

BOLTON CHRONICLE 24th May 1851
"THE PEOPLE'S EXHIBITION CLUB
PATRONS: The Mayor, S. Blair, M.P.,
          Sir Joseph Walmsley M.P.
          The Rev. The Vicar
          Thomas Ridgway Bridson, Esq.
          Thomas Lever Rushton, Esq.

This Club has been formed for enabling the public to visit the Great Exhibition with as little expense as possible, and by it the members of the club will be enabled to go to London and back per rail, and be provided with accommodation to the extent of six beds and six breakfasts, in June for £1.14s and after for £1.9s.

The "Mechanics Home", Ranleigh Road, has been selected by the club as being the most respectable establishment for accommodating the industrious classes. It is situate about a mile from the Great Exhibition building, the new Houses of Parliament, Westminster Abbey, St. James's Park, the Queen's Palace, etc., and in the immediate proximity of Cubits Pimlico Pier, where steamboats arrive from the city every ten minutes.

Every information will be given as to the speediest and cheapest method of visiting the principal Institutions, Public Buildings, and other objects of national interest. Each party will be met at Euston Square Station by an efficient guide.

Payment of Subscriptions: The meetings for receiving subscriptions will be held at the office of the club, No. 11, Commercial Hall, Market Street, every Monday and Thursday evening at seven o'clock, and every Saturday evening at six o'clock, closing at nine each evening. On payment of 2s. 6d. per member, the advantages of the club will be secured.
By order of the Committee
Bolton 16th May 1851   James Swift, Secretary."

The "Mechanics' Home" gave good value for money. One shilling and threepence per night bought a good bed and covering, with towels and soap included. Soups and salads, pork pies and sausages, bacon, cold meats, with pickles, eggs and potatoes, tea and coffee, were amongst the food available. There was a reading room, and a smoking room, with music to entertain the guests between 8 and 9 p.m., as they quaffed their ale or porter.

The fears of the few regarding the probable unruliness of the 'working classes' were completely unfounded. The orderliness and decent behaviour surprised everybody; for the whole 140 days the Exhibition was open there was not one unpleasant incident.

There were some 13,000 exhibits, ranging from a 24-ton block of coal to a thimble, submitted by practically every country in the world. Sculpture, jewellery, beds, reapers, revolvers, and curious inventions were displayed to be admired or scorned as the fancy took.

The Exhibition opened on 1st May and continued until 11th October. The popular period for the visit of Boltonians was August and September. Special trains left on Saturdays and Wednesdays, and the details of numbers travelling were given weekly in the Bolton Chronicle.

Week-ending August 9th	Saturday	63
	Wednesday	52
	Booked	85
Week-ending August 16th	Saturday	170
	Wednesday	70
	Booked	70
Week-ending August 30th	Saturday	86
	Wednesday	59
	Booked	30
Week-ending September 6th	Saturday	55
	Wednesday	97
	Booked	85
Week-ending September 13th	Saturday	110
	Wednesday	142
	Booked	90
Week-ending September 20th	Saturday	136
	Wednesday	109
	Booked	109

6,201,856 people paid £469,115. 13s. to see the Exhibition, which made a profit of £180,000. There was little doubt that it had been an outstanding success.

LEISURE AND PLEASURE

The battle for the enlightenment of the working class, their moral improvement, their conversion to temperance, their self-improvement, continued unabated. The working class, unfortunately, were unco-operative. After a week of hard work they were unenthusiastic at the idea of spending their one free day on self-improvement. The great majority preferred the conviviality of the pub and singing saloon. The puritanical outlook of most influential Boltonians barred the way to offering any acceptable alternatives for enjoyment on a Sunday.

Liberal Robert Heywood in 1855 offered 3 acres of land near Lever Street as a public park, providing a further two similar plots were made available in other parts of the town. This offer came to naught, as had his previous attempts in 1850 to provide a public park. No great endeavour was made to find the two further sites, and there was the usual outcry by people who were horrified at the thought of their quiet neighbourhood being invaded by hordes of the 'working class'. Even if the scheme had been successful its usefulness would have been severely curtailed, because it certainly would have had to be closed on Sundays. So, Bolton retained its reputation as a town destitute of open spaces.

The sanctity of the Sabbath Day was always the insurmountable obstacle to any attempt to provide any acceptable leisure activities. Even the apparently innocent and growing practice of taking a trip on the train to visit relatives was considered a shameful violation of that sanctity. Even more evil was the habit of sending baskets of pigeons by train to be released at distant stations to race back to their home cotes. It was, of course, quite acceptable for the traffic of goods on Sunday – this was 'business.'

One progressive scheme was, however, accepted and proved a huge success:

BOLTON CHRONICLE 20th March 1852
"PUBLIC LIBRARY AND MUSEUM"

"It will have been observed by the official notice which has appeared in our advertising columns that in accordance with the resolution unanimously agreed to at the last Town Council Meeting, the Mayor had directed arrangements to be made for taking on Friday next the decision of the burgesses as to the establishment of a public library and museum in Bolton. The notice has been issued in pursuance of the provisions of an Act 13 and 14 Victoria Chap. 65 by which, on the votes of two thirds of the ratepayers the Council will be empowered to lay a rate of a halfpenny in the pound for the support of the institution named which will be gratuitously open to all classes of the public, whether resident in the borough or resorting thereto.

The motion for applying the provisions of the Act of Parliament was proposed in the Council by a gentleman of decided conservative opinions, it was seconded by an equally decided liberal, and was agreed to without a dissentient voice. But it has, happily, strong and peculiar recommendations of its own to public countenance, for it is no longer a question of can the great mass of the people be trusted with opportunity of self-improvement, but which are the best methods of furnishing such opportunities, and certainly that now offered to the community of Bolton is one of them.

The charge to be levied is remarkably small, the pleasure and advantage to be derived beyond calculation, and the acceptance of the benefits to be obtained is left entirely with the ratepayers. It is a fact reflecting little credit upon the intelligence of this country that of all European States, England is the worst off for such means of gratuitous amusement and instruction as public libraries afford. While there are no fewer than 107 of such institutions in France, 48 in Austria, 44 in Prussia, 17 in Bavaria, 14 even in Belgium, and so on down to 5 in Denmark, there was till very recently, one only so called in Great Britain, and that was the library founded by Humphrey Cheetham in the Borough of Manchester. We have sufficient reliance on the intelligence of the burgesses to believe that they will not hesitate to give their sanction to the proposition now before them and we are satisfied that when that has been done and the preliminaries disposed of, there will be no lack of support in the way of books and material from the more wealthy residents of the town and neighbourhood. It is a measure greatly to the advantage of the manufacturing interests, for whatever improves the working man must be beneficial to the master, and from that quarter the institution will receive, we feel assured, a liberal support."

The burgesses did agree, and the Bolton Chronicle continued the story:

BOLTON CHRONICLE 21st May 1853
"The Bolton Public Library continues to progress in its formation and in general arrangements preparatory to its opening. Many persons expected to have witnessed the opening before now and no doubt the Library and Museum Committee would have had the institution at present in operation, had that been practicable and convenient. Circumstances presented themselves, however, which showed the desireableness of not doing things hastily, and an amount of care and pains was found to be required of which perhaps few people had previously any idea. The two upper rooms of the Exchange having been taken and cleaned for the purpose of the library and subscriptions having been solicited and numerous sums obtained, a very important task had to be performed in the purchasing of books – the result is that at present the Committee are in possession of about 11,000 books – the subscription list announcing contributions to the amount of about £3,100 of which £376. 17s. 11d. is from the working classes."

BOLTON CHRONICLE 8th October 1853
"BOLTON PUBLIC LIBRARY
The Committee have pleasure to announce that the Library and Reading Rooms will be opened to the public on Wednesday the 12th day of October instant.
    Thos. Holden
    G. J. French   Hon. Secs."

The Mayor conducted the official opening ceremony and expressed the hope that artisans and operatives would take advantage of the opportunities provided and that perhaps it would encourage them to spend their winter evenings reading by their own firesides rather than in the alehouses or streets. It is perhaps unfortunate that the Council members and the invited dignitaries did not set an example of temperance at the following celebrations, a fact which did not go unnoticed. A letter to the paper saw "several cases fit for the magistrates' court" following the "drunken revelry".

BOLTON CHRONICLE 15th October 1853
"PUBLIC LIBRARY
The Reference Library has been visited during Thursday and Friday by very large numbers in the middle and higher classes, and on each evening by as many operatives as it could contain. Many of

these were doubtless actuated by motives of mere curiosity but the applications for books were more numerous than the present staff of officers could at all meet."

The demand for books continued unabated, but there was some disappointment for the officials insomuch that the overwhelming demand was for fiction. The working class did again surprise their 'betters' – the borrowed books were treated with great care and very few were lost or damaged.

The blood sports of the earlier part of the 19th century – cock fights, bull baiting, dog fighting – had been made illegal by the 1850s, but cock fighting and dog fighting did continue at clandestine meetings.

BOLTON CHRONICLE 14th August 1852
"DOG FIGHT
A dog fight took place at Black-lane, Radcliffe about a quarter-past four o'clock on Monday morning last which three or four hundred people assembled to witness. A rumour had been afloat that one of these scenes, which it appears are common in the locality in question, was to 'come-off' in the neighbourhood of Little Lever or Radcliffe, and Police-Sergeant Gillett went along with six constables to prevent it. On their arrival at Black-lane they found two dogs fighting in a ring into which the sergeant proceeded and seized one of them, and an end was put to the battle by their being separated. Inquiry was made as to whose property the animals were; and Joseph Fletcher alias 'Owd Patch' of Little Lever claimed one, the other being owned by three men from Bury. These four parties were taken into custody and others of the mob armed themselves with rails from a hedge and stones from a stoneheap, as if intending to make an attack upon the police, which, however, was not done. The prisoners were taken first to Radcliffe and then to Bury, at which latter place they were on the same day brought before the Magistrates and convicted in the penalty of 20s and costs 14s each. The three residing at Bury paid the fines. Fletcher in default was sent to the New Bailey for a month. It has been stated by some that the fight was for £5 a-side; others have said it was for £15 a-side."

The Bolton Chronicle commented in their issue on 29th April 1854 on another amenity available to the Bolton public, and welcomed the inducement to take advantage of the Bolton

Leisure and Pleasure 87

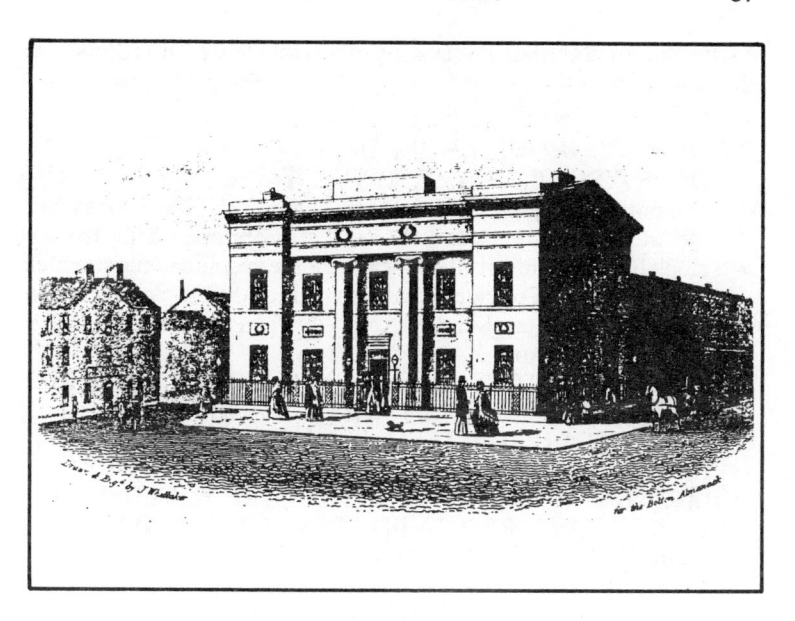

Bolton's new Public Library (*Bolton Almanac*)

Baths in Bridgeman Street by the lowering of admission charges.

BOLTON CHRONICLE 29th April 1854
ADVERTISEMENT – BOLTON BATHS
"The public are respectfully informed that the BATHS consisting of tepid, cold, plunge, and shower baths are open daily from 5 o'clock in the morning until 9 o'clock in the evening in the summer season and from 7 o'clock in the morning until 8 o'clock in the evening in the winter, Sunday excepted, when the hours are until 9 o'clock in the morning.

THE DIRECTORS BEING PERFECTLY SATISFIED THAT GREAT ADVANTAGE TO HEALTH AND COMFORT ARE DERIVED FROM THE PRACTICE OF FREQUENT BATHING, AND BEING DESIROUS OF MAKING THE BOLTON BATHS MORE EXTENSIVELY USEFUL HAVE RESOLVED, FOR THE PRESENT, TO ADOPT THE FOLLOWING LOW SCALE OF CHARGES:

	FIRST CLASS	SECOND CLASS
Cold Plunge	2d	1d
Tepid	6d	3d
Warm Bath	6d	3d
Warm Shower	4d	2d
Cold Shower	2d	1d

The accommodation for the first and second class on the gentlemens as well as the ladies side of the building are perfectly distinct. Towels and dresses are provided on the following terms.

Towels for the first class 1d each; second class ½d each. Dresses for the first class 2d each; second class 1d each.

There is no occasion to give previous notice when hot or tepid baths are required, as the arrangements are such that baths of any temperature can be prepared in a few minutes."

Progress in the provision of amenities for leisure and pleasure was slowly being made, despite the problems of alcoholism and Sabbatarianism. The Corporation had made the first move in acknowledging that they had some responsibility in this sphere by providing a public library; liberal minded mill owners who provided institutes and facilities for leisure activities for their employees saw their amenities more widely used once the emphasis on self-improvement was abandoned. For the most part the working class man was not seeking cultural uplift in his few leisure hours, but a comfortable environment in which to meet his friends, drink a glass of ale, smoke his pipe and read his paper.

RELIGION

Within the boundaries of the Bolton Poor Law Union there were listed in the Bolton Directory for 1853 the following numbers of places of worship:

The Established Church of England	27
Catholic Churches	2
Dissenting Chapels	
Baptist	1
Independent	11
Friends Meeting House	1
Methodist New Connection	1
Presbyterian	1
Unitarian	6
Wesleyan Methodists	26
Wesleyan Refuge	1
Primitive Methodists	5
New Jerusalem	2

The high number of dissenting chapels indicates Bolton's continuing adherence to non-conformity. The middle-class and the higher echelons of the working class were the backbone of both chapel and church, and regular attendance was a necessary part of the social structure. The Parish Church tended to be the preserve of the conservative hierarchy and it was not uncommon to transfer from the Wesleyan Chapel to the Parish Church as one's status in the community improved – both church and chapel were evangelical in outlook and practice.

A census of Church attendance taken on Sunday, 30th March 1851 revealed that 7,333,564 went to church on that day, whilst 5,288,294 able to attend failed to do so. It can safely be assumed that the bulk of the five million non-attenders were members of the lower orders of the working class.

The class structure of the congregation attending the Parish

Church was evidently so obvious that the then Vicar considered it necessary to try and persuade his working class parishioners that there was a place for them.

BOLTON CHRONICLE 10th October 1857
"SERVICES FOR THE WORKING CLASS AT THE PARISH CHURCH
A series of weeknight services specially adapted to the working classes have been arranged by the Rev. the Vicar, the first of which will take place in about a fortnight.

The Rev. gentleman is anxious to enlist the sympathy of the working classes for those great principles of religion, which enable and dignify human nature, but which vast numbers of them have hitherto entirely lost sight of. The usual church service, we understand, will be considerably curtailed in order to allow more time for the address from the pulpit."

BOLTON CHRONICLE 24th October 1857
"THE SPECIAL SERVICES AT THE PARISH CHURCH FOR THE WORKING CLASSES.
The first of the series of six special services for the working classes took place on Thursday evening when the Parish Church was densely crowded in every part, hundreds standing and hundreds more unable to gain admission. The bulk of those present were men and women of the working classes, no children being admitted, and though the majority were attired in their working dress, all appeared clean and decent."

One reaction to this experiment is voiced in a letter to the Editor of the Bolton Chronicle dated 5th December 1857:

"THE SPECIAL SERVICES IN THE PARISH CHURCH.
– I accordingly went and I think I have never heard a sermon that was better adapted to secure the end in view. It was so plain, simple and straight-forward, and adorned with an eloquence I have very seldom heard in a minister of the Gospel, and at the conclusion he earnestly invited all parties, and particularly the working classes, to attend the church or some other place of worship. He asked them to come and fill the pews, and when the pews were filled they could fill the aisles, and then they could build more churches. Now all this is very good and as it ought to be, but how is it carried out in practice? Being so well pleased I determined to accept the Vicar's invitation and accordingly I mentioned it to two friends who agreed to accompany me. We went the Sunday morning following. We saw the gentleman of the gown whose duty it is to find strangers seats – he told us to wait a few moments – we waited until the service

commenced but he never returned. I was consulting with my friends as to the propriety of going away when another gentleman of the gown made his appearance, and having solicited him he condescended to take us to some benches close to the wall, where it was impossible to see the minister and very difficult to hear him. I should not have thought anything about this had there not been plenty of pews that were not more than half full.

I came out of the church quite disappointed at the treatment we received, because it was so much different to what I expected from what the Vicar had said. Now I think the Vicar must not be aware that his servants use people in this way or he would never have given the invitation he does to all parties to attend the church.
A third working man."

The 'gentleman of the gown' duly replied to this complaint:

BOLTON CHRONICLE 12th December 1857
"Sirs,
Seeing in your paper of Saturday last a letter signed "A third working man", complaining of the want of attention and courtesy of the apparitors of the Parish Church, we deem it our duty to say that our conduct has always been the opposite to that which your correspondent complains of. We do not deny that it is possible that after he had been promised a seat by one of the 'gentlemen of the gown' as he terms them, he never returned to conduct them to the promised accommodation, but we do most emphatically deny that this was intentional. With respect to his complaint relative to another of the apparitors conducting him and his two friends to some benches close to the wall we would ask where did this "Third Working Man" desire a seat? Does he want the same privileges as the pew-holders?

May we be permitted to remark that he who comes to the house of prayer to 'worship in spirit and in truth' cares little about the seat if he can hear and thereby join in the devotional services.

We should indeed be sorry if our conduct in any manner thwarted the good intentions of the Vicar in his endeavours to secure the attendance of working men at the church. Every stranger visiting St. Peters may rest assured that the utmost care and attention to their comfortable accommodation will ever be paid by,
     Sirs,
      Yours etc,
       J. Booth
       J. Horrocks Apparitors."

Probably the greatest talking point in 1851 apart from the

Religion

The Parish Church (*Bolton Almanac*)

Great Exhibition was the proposal by the Pope to divide England into Roman Catholic dioceses, following on the earlier announcement that Archbishop Wiseman, the leading Roman Catholic in England, was to be made a Cardinal.

Roman Catholicism had been accepted with the Catholic Emancipation Act of 1829, which had accorded the status of civic equality to all those of that faith. A large proportion of the Protestant population still opposed this acceptance, and as could be expected from the people of Bolton numerous outbursts of vehement protest appeared over the years in the local press. Parliament did try to quieten the outcry with the "Ecclesiastical Titles Bill", which made it illegal for Catholics to call themselves English Bishops. Nothing happened and the Bill was repealed in 1872.

The Bolton Chronicle referred to the Catholic 'problem' at frequent periods, and an editorial in January 1853 regarding the treatment of Protestants in Tuscany, followed its usual line:

> "Popery is unchanged and unchangeable. Its real character is masked in England, where its progress would be at once arrested if only it dared to display itself in all its hideous deformity and atrocious terrorism. Where Romanism has the opportunity, where its spiritual despotism is backed by the subserviency of the civil power, where public opinion is gagged, where the press is fettered or silenced, where the mass of the people are thoroughly indoctrinated by Jesuit bigots, there we find the reading of the Word of Life interdicted as a crime against the State; there we find those who even privately seek to derive consolation from the fountain of scriptural truth are liable to be dragged from their homes and immured in loathsome dungeons."

The Roman Catholics of Bolton thought it fit and necessary that they should take action to 'obtain their just rights' and formed the Bolton Catholic Defence Association. A report of their Annual General Meeting appeared in the Bolton Chronicle dated 23rd April 1853. The Chairman in his opening remarks asserted:

> "They (Bolton Catholics) wished to be placed upon an equality with others and for his own part he would not be content with less. The Association had materially aided in securing the return of two Catholic gentlemen to the Board of Guardians; one for Great Bolton and the other for Little Bolton, each Township now having a Catholic to represent the poor Catholics of the town, where they

were formerly without even one to defend their rights. Mr. Councillor Parkinson in his supporting remarks said: Some people would ask why it was requisite that there should be a Catholic Defence Association, when other religious sects did not consider anything of the kind necessary on their part. The fact was that all other religious bodies were tolerated to any amount. No matter how they were opposed to one another, as long as they agreed on what they considered essentials they tolerate in one another the greatest amount of absurdity; but the Catholics were made an object of attack. Unlike every other religious denomination the Catholics were marked out in an especial manner. It was necessary to have such an Association because at a time when they hoped bigotry had to a great extent died away, people belonging to the Church of England, so called, Wesleyans, Independents and all the other various sects could be brought together to spit upon the poor 'Papish'. Was it not desirable that some species of machinery should be called into existence to be in readiness to put in motion when it was required that the Catholics should assert their rights? Was it not requisite that steps should be taken for placing every Catholic who was entitled to it by the amount of rent he paid, on the list of voters for members of Parliament? Was it wise, or otherwise, that every Catholic in the Borough should claim upon rental and rating to be placed on the burgess list to vote for men to take part in the spending of their money, as well as the public money, in the Council Chamber."

Religion played an important part in the lives of about half the population of Bolton, whether it be a sincere act of faith, or just part of the required social strata. The other half were untouched by Christian teaching, but were concerned with the struggle for survival and could see no help forthcoming from Church or Chapel except exhortation to work harder and accept their station in life.

POLITICS

The 1832 Reform Bill and the 1835 Municipal Reform Bill had gone some way to removing the complete authority of the Church and wealthy landowners. The 1832 Reform Bill extended the right to vote in Parliamentary elections to owners of property with a rateable value of £10 and above – male only of course. Even this extension only increased the electoral roll to include one out of six of the male population, but it did get rid of thinly populated country boroughs, and gave representation to the new industrial towns of the north, which had previously been unrepresented in Parliament.

The Municipal Reform Bill allowed the vote to elect members to the town or borough councils to those householders who had occupied their property for three years or more and had paid the poor rate.

Neither Bill made any provision for ballots to be made in secret; every voter had publicly to declare his allegiance to either the Conservative or Liberal cause. Consequently the way was wide open for bribery and corruption. The wealthier artisan was cautioned that his future employment was at stake if his political views varied from those of his employer; the merchant and shopkeeper was reminded where his best interests lay; cash payments for votes were made, and ale and liquor flowed freely on Election Day. The requirements of the Municipal Reform Bill allowed manipulation of the electoral roll to aid the election of a favoured candidate. Bolton, despite its claim to some moral and spiritual elevation, was no example of the correct and democratic way to elect Parliamentary and municipal members.

The Bolton Chronicle was totally committed to the Conservative cause, and the result of the July 1852 Parliamentary election brought forth caustic comment:

BOLTON CHRONICLE 17th July 1852
"ELECTION RESULT

Barnes	(Liberal)	745
Crook	(Liberal)	727
Blair	(Conservative)	717
Ainsworth	(Conservative)	345

Editorial Comment
The rejection, by a majority of ten votes, of a gentleman, unexceptionable in private character and public reputation, pledged to fair and reasonable political progress, and member of a Church guaranteeing unvarying protection to Protestant interests of every kind alike, for a candidate of whom nothing is known but the extreme violence of the political and other principles he professes in opposition to every class and *creed*, whatever in his case that may be except his own, is an achievement upon which, on due reflection, we believe the great body of the electors of Bolton will scarcely find room to congratulate themselves. The Liberals of Bolton must know, if they will let their judgement overcome their prejudice, that under a constitution such as we happily possess, the revolutionary changes which Messrs. Barnes and Crook are pledged to bring about are utterly impossible. So long as the present form of government is to be maintained; the present equitable balance of influence preserved to the three estates of the realm, the policy of raising the power of the working classes upon the subjugation and ruin of every other class cannot be pursued. To attempt it is to commence revolution, and that is the whole meaning of what Messrs. Barnes and Crook have promised 'the masses' in return for their support. "I go to Parliament", says Mr. Barnes, "only for destruction, your present rulers are jews and robbers. I will do nothing but oppose, thwart, obstruct the legislation of the country, because I will do nothing but drive the Ministry from office." What is this but useless, hollow, disgraceful factionness?

On the other side, had Mr. Blair been placed at the head of the poll, as he might and should have been, he would have returned to Parliament to help forward measures of value that can be accomplished.

Mr. Crook's theory of equality is worse than ridiculous, for it is wilful delusion, a snare to entrap the ignorant into giving power to their self constituted leaders for personal and selfish objects only.

He (Mr. Blair) would have gone to promote by practical means the religion, the education, the health, the peace and prosperity of the people, in their truest sense. Messrs. Barnes and Crook go to join a minority for opposition sake alone, and a miserable faction in the house for the furtherance of revolutionary changes, which can never be affected, as their particular purpose."

The election of Messrs. Barnes and Crook brought forth a storm of protest and accusations of coercion, bribery and befuddlement, and resulted in a petition being presented to Parliament.

"*BOLTON PETITION 4th December 1852*
To the honourable the Commons of the United Kingdom of Great Britain and Ireland, in Parliament assembled. The humble petition of the undersigned George Greenhalgh of Bolton-le-Moors, in the County of Lancaster, a registered elector of the said Borough, and had right to vote and did vote at the said election.

That at the said election Thomas Barnes, Esq., Joseph Crook, Esq., Stephen Blair, Esq., and Peter Ainsworth, Esq., were candidates and that a poll being demanded the same was granted and proceeded with and at the close thereof the election was declared by the returning officer to have fallen upon the said Thomas Barnes and Joseph Crook, who were accordingly returned as members duly elected to serve in the present Parliament for the said Borough of Bolton-le-Moors.

That before, at, and during the said election, the said Thomas Barnes and Joseph Crook were, and each of them, was by themselves, their agents, managers, friends, and partisans, respectively guilty of many acts of bribery and corruption, in order to corrupt and procure, and did, and each of them did, by their said agents, managers, friends and partisans, and by other persons employed on their behalf, by gifts, presents, money, rewards, and by threats, intimidation, undue influence, and by other corrupt and illegal practices, acts and means, corrupt and procure diverse persons, having and claiming to have votes at the said election, to give their votes for them the said Thomas Barnes and Joseph Crook, or one of them, and to forbear to give their votes in favour of the said Stephen Blair.

That the said Thomas Barnes and Joseph Crook by the said corrupt and illegal practices were and are wholly incapacitated and ineligible to serve in this present Parliament for the said Borough and the said election and return of the said Thomas Barnes and Joseph Crook were and are wholly null and void."

To the disgust of the Bolton Chronicle, the Committee elected to consider the petition rejected the complaints and confirmed the right of Messrs. Barnes and Crook to continue to represent the Borough in Parliament.

BOLTON CHRONICLE 7th May 1853
"*THE BOLTON ELECTION PETITION*
The result of the petition praying for an inquiry into the return of the sitting members of this Borough has both disappointed and astonished the public. After a brief investigation the Committee have come to the decision that Messrs. Barnes and Crook have been duly elected and that the petition against their return was 'frivolous and vexatious'.

Of course the Conservative party never could have anticipated that such a result was ever within the 'chapter of accidents', or they would have prosecuted the petition. We have valid reasons for believing that the issue was equally unexpected by the Radicals themselves, for it was clear from the statements made by the parties who were subpoenaed as witnesses in support of the allegations of the petition, that a system of bribery, intimidation and corruption had prevailed in the borough on the occasion of the last election.

We are aware that this is not the conclusion to which the Committee have arrived. It may be that legally and technically speaking, sufficient evidence was not adduced to warrant the unseating of the members, but after a careful investigation of the testimony of all witnesses, we feel justified in maintaining that the Conservatives had a very strong ground for presenting the petition, and that the charge of bribery appears to have been conclusively established in more than one distinct case. The evidence will speak for itself. It will show that Bolton is not exempt from those corrupt practices which have excited so much attention during the present session of Parliament. We have amongst us, parties who are as capable of being bought and sold as many of the 'potwallopers' under the old system of close boroughs, and (must it not be added) we have amongst us men who will degrade themselves and debase the constituency by purchasing the suffrages of the election. The charges of bribery and corruption are not one whit the less true because it has not been sufficiently supported to satisfy a doubtful tribunal of its existence in what the tribunal considers a legal and constitutional manner, nor will these practices the less forcibly recoil upon the guilty heads of those who resort to them but have secured a temporary but inglorious triumph."

On the 14th May 1853 the Editor of the Bolton Chronicle still remained concerned with the result of the enquiry of alleged bribery and corruption during the Parliamentary election campaign, and wrote at length on the corrupt electoral system, but condemned any thought of reform by way of introducing the "secret ballot".

"What can be more startling to the believer in the political purity of the present generation, than the fact that eighty-five petitions against the return of members at the last general election have been sent up this session? That in almost every case the petitions have alleged bribery, treating, intimidation and sometimes all the three, against the sitting member or his agents, or both, and that, owing to the difficulty of obtaining evidence even where evil practices are known to have taken place, and the great cost of establishing evidence even when obtained, these 85 petitions do not represent one half of the corruption which prevailed last July.

". . . And then as to the [secret] ballot. Does anybody really believe that men who bribe and who receive bribes, with the dread of exposure and its consequences before them, will become all at once pure in heart, when every chance of detection is removed? The thing is absurd. "Oh, but" say its advocates "no man will be fool enough to give a bribe when he does not know that the man who receives it will vote for him". Certainly not. But men have given and, it is fair to presume, will give money for a seat in Parliament. Under the ballot they will experience no difficulty – "Birds of a feather flock together", and the men whose votes are saleable know each other and have their leader or spokesman. In nineteen cases out of twenty their votes will turn the election. What more easy, therefore, than to bargain for a certain sum conditionally? Mr. Placehunter wants a seat and will give £1000 for it. Thomas Turnpenny says to the two hundred voters under his management, "If Mr. P is returned my lads, there'll be a five a-piece for us". Can any one doubt the result? Well might a thorough electioneering agent exclaim "Give me the ballot and a bag of sovereigns and I will carry any election in the United Kingdom".

Wherein then is the true remedy for this frightful state of affairs, does the reader ask? The answer is not difficult. Render the exposure of corrupt practices easy and cheap, instead of cumbrous and costly. In all cases punish heavily the agent or agents upon detection. Disfranchise at once, and for ever, every voter concerned directly, in the giving or receiving of bribes. But this after all is mere tinkers work, having the merit of being a little more effectual and practical than the Reform panacea. The great and the only thorough remedy is one slow in its operation. It is the elevation of the character of the constituency. It is impossible by arbitrary legislation to root out corruption from our electoral system, so long as there are voters who are so poor and so ignorant as to think a sovereign a better thing than a pure conscience. The great thing, then is to introduce an educational qualification; to improve the constituency by swelling the numbers of those who believe that the franchise is a sacred trust, for the honest and faithful discharge of which they are responsible to God and their Country. Education, and above all, a religious education, is the great purifier. Once open a man's eyes to the social and political importance of the vote he holds; once make him feel that to sell it to the highest bidder, is to injure his fellow man and sin against his own soul; and the briber may practise his dirty arts in vain. We dare say all this will sound very antiquated and foolish in Radical ears, but we cannot help it. We have a greater reverence for religion even than for reform. We are old fashioned enough to believe that the man who fears God, and who does unto his neighbours as he would have his neighbours do unto him, will not be a bad citizen. And if to religion he adds knowledge, political and historical, we think he is likely to be an honest and trustworthy voter. If he possesses not these qualifications, then for all political purposes he is a minor, and should be treated accordingly. A man ignorant of the importance of the franchise and careless about its exercise, should no more be trusted with the franchise than should an infant with a razor."

The results of the Municipal elections in November 1852 did nothing to relieve the apprehensions of the Editor of the Bolton Chronicle.

BOLTON CHRONICLE 6th November 1852
"The Election on Monday last of twelve councillors to represent six wards in the Borough was a matter of more interest than any municipal election in Bolton has been for some years past. The Liberal Party, flushed by their success at the late Parliamentary election, determined to take every possible means to secure the position they had attained, and considered it by no means the least important that the management of the municipal affairs should be in their hands. They, therefore, set to work in good time, in great earnest, and with much energy, and partly in consequence of previous organisation, and partly from subsequent exertions, they formed a combination calculated to do a great work. The Conservatives followed the example of organising and bestirred themselves in a manner that evinced no small degree of spirit on their part, and, though they had not the advantage of the operations which their opponents had carried on for years, an amount of determination manifested itself which intimated that the contest of November 1852, would be a most lively one. And so it proved to be. The Burgess roll had become considerably extended over its limits of former years; a much greater number of voters had to poll than on any previous occasion; and more machinery for the conducting of an election was needed. An active bustling scene was created, and excitement presented itself on every hand. The result, as many of our readers know, has been the defeat of the

Conservatives, four of their candidates and eight of the Liberals being returned to the Council; and a further consequence has been great exultation in Liberal quarters. There have been trumpetings of victory, boasting of success and denunciations of the defeated; and, to hear a Radical talk, a simple minded person would be led to the belief that Liberalism must prevail, and Conservatism forthwith sink into the dust. The Liberals would have it believed that they have won the election because the Bolton Conservatives have squandered the ratepayers money in extravagance and involved the Borough in almost inextricable difficulties, and because morality, truth and economy are on the side of the Liberals, while nothing but wastefulness, corruption and mismanagement connect themselves with conservatism. So goes the story of the Liberals interested in the movements of Monday last – but much different are the facts. The Conservatives have not lost the election because they have been wasteful or incompetent to deal with the affairs of the borough, or because they have been guilty of 'jobbery'. One very great reason for their losing has been that these things have been 'believed'; that they have been crammed down people's throats with enormous force; that falsehoods of the grossest kind have been circulated and foul aspersions and misrepresentation disseminated with a zeal that would have done credit to a better cause. The success of the Liberals is largely attributable to their perfect organisation, but more largely to the unscrupulous means of which they have availed themselves by barefacedly stating that the Tories had done things which they themselves had done, and of which some of the more important of their Party openly signify their approval. A new market is being erected on a large and creditable scale, the cost of which, incurred by Liberals as well as Conservatives, is endeavoured to be made into a matter of odium, as is also the case in regard to waterworks extension, and street and sewerage improvements. The most extraordinary feature of the sequel to Monday's proceedings has been the efforts put forth to paint the Conservatives in colours and the Liberals with tints of the veriest innocence and virtue. "Purity of election" is said to have won the victory and 'independent electors' and 'honest men' are represented as those who achieved it; while everything that is bad is laid to the charge of the defeated. If 'purity' consists of buying Liberal votes at various prices up to 20s or 30s each, it has had a part in the matter, for such things were done on Monday last, as were a host of others in a like category, an enumeration of which would occupy more room than we can spare. To briefly notice a few of these 'honest' transactions, it may be stated that Liberal drink was, on Sunday and Monday, given to a very great extent; Liberal voters were brought to vote in a state of intoxication; Conservatives were threatened with instant dismissal from their employment if they voted not for Liberal candidates; voters pledged to support Conservative candidates were treated to brute force, had voting papers snatched from their hands or torn by Liberal councillors, Liberal mill-owners and others of the same school. Conservative burgesses have been personated (in Church ward alone to the number of 7) and conservative shopkeepers have been menaced by bodies of people with threats of exclusive dealing. A certain victualling house (whence on Sunday afternoon, during Divine service, a Conservative passer-by was taunted about his Bible and a jeer was used about 'burning it') was filled on Sunday evening with company who could have any quantity of Liberal drink, free of expense, a number of persons who were pledged to vote conservative being 'bottled'. Amongst the intimidated we have a number of men who are actually members of the Operative Conservative Association and were compelled to vote against their principles. One man that we hear of was out of work, and as an inducement to vote on the Liberal side was promised employment at a certain cotton mill. The work was provided for him on Monday, but that day being over and his vote recorded the work was discontinued and was succeeded by disappointment. To speak of persons who were not coerced by their employers, it might be stated that in one Ward alone (Bradford) there were sufficient to have changed the number of votes polled so as to have secured the return of one or both Conservative candidates, had the 'screw' not been applied by their masters."

The Municipal elections of 1855 and 1858 gave no joy to the Bolton Chronicle – the Liberals were still winning seats on the Council.

BOLTON CHRONICLE 3rd November 1855
"*TOWN COUNCIL*
The first of November has again passed without any united effort being made to return on that day a body of men qualified by education, business training, intelligence and social standing.

Someday, we venture to prophesy, our townsmen who are now slumbering so complacently, will be rudely drive out of their fool's paradise. Large interests like those now committed to the care of the Town Council, cannot be well and wisely conducted by the noisy nobodies who are fast usurping all municipal power."
BOLTON CHRONICLE 6th November 1858
"*THE MUNICIPAL ELECTION*
We are gratified to perceive the increased interest manifested in our local affairs, though we must confess, that gratification is considerably qualified by the consideration that the filthy and

degrading, and let us add, dishonourable practices of bribery, treating and personation, were only too prevalent during the elections. It must be a source of disgust, regret and indignation to every well regulated and honest mind to find that many persons from whom a greatly better and superior line of conduct might reasonably have been expected, did not only consider it no wrong to resort to means for debasing and degrading their fellow burgesses, but that they should almost take a pride in pursuing a course so derogatory to their own character and position. We feel that there is no language too strong to denounce the bribers and the bribed, the treaters and the treated. We trust that means will be devised by the legislature for putting a stop to these disgraceful practices."

There was little joy for the Editor of the Bolton Chronicle in the Parliamentary Election of 1857 when Captain William Gray under the banner of 'Liberal-Conservative' was elected along with the Liberal Joseph Crook and in 1859 the same two were returned unopposed – the Conservatives had evidently retired from the fray. It wasn't until 1865 that Bolton returned a Conservative member of Parliament; at that election William Gray, now Lieut-Colonel, topped the Poll as a 'Conservative' without any 'Liberal' attachment.

MEDICINE

In the 1850s new ideas in the field of medicine and surgery were, like other ideas of reform, slowly being accepted and practised.

An Act of 1832 had legalised the increase in the supply of bodies to the various schools of anatomy, which previously had depended on the illegal supply provided, at a price, by the gangs of 'body-snatchers', or the more poetically named 'resurrection-men'. Knowledge increased apace, and with that knowledge came pamphlets and papers on a variety of conditions and treatments, but conservative members of the medical profession were loath to accept 'new fangled' ideas.

One such innovation was the use of anaesthetic, which had been suggested as early as 1800 by Humphrey Davy. Successful operations depended on the speed at which the surgeon could work on the patient bound to the operating table by rope or held down by strong assistants. Even where the surgeon performed with the required speed and skill, the shock of the intense pain could kill the patient. Even having survived the ordeal, infection caused by unhygienic instruments and conditions added further to the mortality figures. Despite the obvious advantages of anaesthetizing the patient, many surgeons frowned on the idea and thought it an affront to their skill, and considered the use of chloroform would result in more fatalities. Clergy and lay people joined in the condemnation, and claimed that to avert pain by artificial means was against the will of God. One professor did, however, hit back at these critics by pointing out that God himself put Adam to sleep before removing the rib to create Eve.

It was Queen Victoria who inspired the general acceptance of the use of anaesthetics. On 7th April 1853 she gave birth to her eighth child, aided by the use of chloroform. The previous seven births had been painful and exhausting, but with the aid of what she described as "blessed chloroform" she was "soothed and quietened beyond measure". So, with Royal approval, chloroform was accepted and in general use by 1857.

The Medical Act of 1858 regulated the training and discipline of Doctors, and made provision for the establishment of a register of qualified Medical Practitioners. With all the advancement most could not afford the Doctor's fee, and relied on home remedies, and the multitude of 'quack' pills and medicines which were readily available for a few pence. Fretful and sickly children were quietened by a dose of the popular "Godfrey's Cordial", a mixture of laudanum and syrup, which was effective enough, but too large a dose was lethal, and repeated smaller doses only postponed the final solution. Another tranquillizer for a poorly child was to add liberal quantitities of gin to the child's milk. For every known ailment the Bolton Chronicle carried advertisements which claimed a cure.

BOLTON CHRONICLE 24th December 1852
"OLD DR. JACOB TOWNSEND'S GREAT AMERICAN SARSAPARILLA
This celebrated medicine was originally discovered in the year 1805, and is the only genuine Townsend's Sarsaparilla in England or America.

With nearly 50 years trial on the most inveterate Chronic Maladies, it has proved itself a medicine of unexampled virtue and value to mankind. Composed as it is of all the rarest roots, herbs, flowers, buds and seeds of plants that grow on American soil, with sarsaparilla as the base, it holds in combination a greater amount of medicinal virtue than any other medicine known to the world.

Its design is to act upon the blood, and through that, upon all the organs and tissues of the system. It has been so prepared that it partakes very much of the gastric juice of the stomach, and does in consequence enter directly in the vital current, thus creating –
NEW, PURE, AND RICH BLOOD.

It wonderfully aids weak, impaired and debilitated organs, invigorates the nervous system, tones up and strengthens the digestive apparatus, and imparts new life and vigour to all functions of the body. A cure for Dyspepsia, weal, sour and irritable stomachs, Headache, Jaundice, pain in the side, Eruptions and blotches of the skin, weakness and debility.

Calculated to cure Scrofula, Erysypelas, Mercurial diseases, Scorbutic eruptions; the same is true in respect to Rheumatism, Gout, Pains in the bones, Piles, Fistula, Sore eyes, Ulcer sores, and is particularly calculated to remove all complaints peculiar to children such as Quinsey, Sore throat, Croup, Whooping Cough, Measles, Bowel complaints, Cholera Infantuar, Scarlet Fever, and the whole train of infantile diseases.

But in no department is it more valuable and efficacious than in the cure of disease peculiar to females –

Falling of the womb, Fluor Albos, Pains in the back, hips and loins, and great distress in the head, great weakness, palpitation of the Heart, and Mental depression, painful suppressed or excessive Menses.

ALL THESE COMPLAINTS OLD DOCTOR TOWNSEND'S SARSAPARILLA WILL COMPLETELY REMOVE AND RESTORE THE PARTY TO HEALTH AND ENJOYMENT OF LIFE.

PINTS 4s.   SMALL QUARTS 4s.6d.
IMPERIAL QUARTS 7s.6d."

Parr's Life Pills, Holloway's Ointments and Pills, Norris's Drops and Battley's Sedative, were but a few of the wondrous remedies available to the readers of the Bolton Chronicle.

Death was such a commonplace event that the fact that many of the remedial pills and concoctions contained opium, sulphuric acid, and similar poisons, and after large doses or long usage did affect an all too permanent cure, raised no surprise or comment.

Bolton had made some real provision for the chronic sick and injured with the erection in 1823 of a "commodious stone building, with a handsome free-stone frontage" to house an Infirmary and Dispensary, in Nelson Square, off Bradshawgate. The institution was maintained by subscription, and a comprehensive report was given at the Annual General Meeting in 1851.

BOLTON CHRONICLE 8th March 1851
"BOLTON INFIRMARY AND DISPENSARY
The annual meeting of the subscribers was held in the Committee Room of the institution on Thursday forenoon last. The Chairman (Rev. J. Slade) commenced proceedings by reading the following report.

NEVER FAILING REMEDY.

HOLLOWAY'S OINTMENT.

CURE OF A CRIPPLE AFTER 10 YEARS' SUFFERING.

Extract from a Letter from Mr. John Thompson, Chemist, Liverpool, dated August 20th 1852.

To Professor Holloway.

DEAR SIR,—I am enabled to furnish you with a most extraordinary cure effected by your invaluable Ointment and Pills, which has astonished every person acquainted with the sufferer. About 10 years ago, Mr. W. Cummins, of Saltney-street, in this town, was thrown from his horse, whereby he received very serious injuries; he had the best medical advice at the time, and was afterwards an inmate of different infirmaries, yet he grew worse, at length a malignant running ulcer settled in his hip, which so completely crippled him, that he could not move without crutches for nearly 10 years; recently he began to use your Ointment and Pills, which have now healed the wound, strengthened the limb, and enabled him to dispense with his crutches, so that he can walk with the greatest of ease, and with renewed health and vigour. (Signed) J. THOMPSON.

The Pills should be used conjointly with the Ointment in most of the following cases:

Bad Legs	Chiego-foot	Fistulas	Sore Throats
Bad Breasts	Chilblains	Gout	Skin Diseases
Burns	Chapped Hands	Glandular Swellings	Scurvy
Bunions	Corns (soft)	Lumbago	Sore Heads
Bite of Moschetoes and Sand-Flies	Cancers	Piles	Tumours
	Contracted and Stiff Joints	Rheumatism	Ulcers
		Scalds	Wounds
Coco-Bay	Elephantiasis	Sore Nipples	Yaws

Sold by the Proprietor 244, Strand (near Temple Bar), London, and by all respectable Vendors of Patent Medicines throughout the civilized World, in Pots and Boxes, at 1s. 1½d., 2s. 9d., 4s. 6d., 11s., 22s., and 33s. each. There is a considerable saving in taking the larger sizes.

N.B.—Directions for the guidance of Patients are affixed to each Pot.

Steam Engines—Watt's first patent, 1769; Ditto for double engine, 1781.

One of Holloway's remedies (*Bolton Almanac*)

HEALTH FOR A SHILLING.

HOLLOWAY'S PILLS.

EXTRAORDINARY CURE OF LOSS OF HEALTH—DISORDERED STOMACH—INDIGESTION AND DETERMINATION OF BLOOD TO THE HEAD.

Copy of a Letter from Mr. John Lloyd, of Erw-wen, near Harlech, Merionethshire.

To Professor Holloway.

Sir,—I avail myself of the first opportunity of informing you, that for a very long period I was afflicted with a dangerous giddiness and frequent swimmings in the head, attended by loss of appetite disordered stomach, and generally impaired health. Every means had failed to give me any permanent relief, and at length it became so alarming that I was really afraid of going about without an attendant. In this melancholy condition I waited personally upon Mr. Hughes, Chemist, Harleach, for the purpose of consulting him as to what I had better do; he kindly recommended your Pills, I tried them without delay, and after taking them for a short time I am happy to bear testimony to their wonderful efficacy. I am now restored to perfect health, and enabled to resume my usual duties. You are quite at liberty to publish this letter in any way you may think proper.

I am, Sir, your obedient Servant (Signed), JOHN LLOYD.
June 6th, 1852.   Erw-wen, Harlech, Merionethsire.

These celebrated Pills are wonderfully efficacious in the following complaints:

Ague	Dropsy	Jaundice	Secondary Symptoms
Asthma	Dysentery	Liver Complaints	
Bilious Complaints	Erysipelas	Lumbago	Tic Douloureux
Blotches on the Skin	Female Irregularities	Piles	Tumours
		Rheumatism	Ulcers
Bowel Complaints	Fevers of all kinds	Retention of Urine	Venereal Affections
Colics	Fits		
Constipation of Bowels	Gout	Sc.ofula or King's Evil	Worms of all kinds
	Head-aches		Weakness, from whatever cause, &c., &c.
Consumption	Indigestion	Sore Throats	
Debility	Inflammation	Stone and Gravel	

Sold at the Establishment of Professor HOLLOWAY, 244, Strand (near Temple Bar) London, and by all respectable Druggists and Dealers in Medicines throughout the Civilized World, at the following prices:—1s. 1½d., 2s. 9d., 4s 6d., 11s, 22s., and 33s. each box. There is a considerable saving by taking the larger sizes.—*Directions for the guidance of Patients in every disorder are affixed to each Box.*

Savings Banks under parliamentary regulation, 1816; extended to Scotland; 1835.

Another Holloway's remedy (*Bolton Almanac*)

Patients Admitted and Discharged

Ordinary Patients admitted since March 7th 1850	– 1151
Home Patients admitted since March 7th 1850	– 999
In Patients admitted since March 7th 1850	– 24
Remaining on books March 7th 1850	– 244
	2418

ORDINARY PATIENTS DISCHARGED

Cured	– 1154
Relieved	– 52
Irregular	– 24
Transferrred to Union	– 5
Own request	– 4
Dead	– 29

HOME PATIENTS DISCHARGED		IN-PATIENTS DISCHARGED
Cured	664	12
Relieved	49	5
Irregular	26	–
Transferred to Union	66	1
Own Request	–	–
Dead	109	3

Receipts for the year – £42.3s.2d.
In hand at commencement – £722.2s.4d.

The expenditure comprised a number of ordinary items, as money paid for drugs, House Surgeon and Dispenser's Salaries, amounting together to £680.13s.10d. A balance remained in the Bank on March 1st 1851 of £41.8s.6d.

REPORT The Committee desire to draw the attention of the subscribers and the public to their annual report and respectfully entreat them to favourably consider the statement here made respecting this excellent and important Institution. There can be no question whatever that it renders, as it always has done, incalculable benefit to the industrial classes of this Borough. Of whatever improvements it may be capable, whatever objections may be entertained against the working of any of its departments, no person can deny that it is the most efficient, comprehensive and extensive charity in this populous community, in proportion to its means.

The Infirmary department, to which attention has been

frequently drawn, is still exceedingly defective, is doing comparatively nothing for want of adequate support, and it never can be properly available till some steps are taken for its enlargement; such a step is now more than ever required as admissions into the Manchester Infirmary become more and more difficult and uncertain. Many cases now treated at home need a better attendance and more experienced nursing of an infirmary, and the friends of the poor, and the masters of large establishments would do well to give the subject their serious and immediate consideration. The infirmary is open to the whole neighbourhood, and therefore the whole neighbourhood is deeply concerned.

We have in conclusion a bounden duty to discharge, always a pleasing duty, to express the great obligation under which this Institution has to all the Honorary Medical Officers for the skill and vigilance and kindness which the patients receive at their hands, upon which both the credit and usefulness of the Charity so materially depend, and of the House Surgeon also we can testify that he has shown in the performance of his duty an assiduity with which the subscribers have reason to be satisfied.

Mr. Taylor said that in his experience as Coroner he has found during the last two or three years, that death sometimes occurred from the want of immediate attention to cases of accident, owing in some degree to the unwillingness of poor persons to obtain the assistance of Union surgeons, and it appears to him desirable that, as suggested, the Infirmary should be extended in order that such cases might oftener be taken there and the sufferers receive timely aid.

The resolution having been shaped as follows was unanimously adopted –

That the Committee be empowered and required to furnish additional wards with six beds for surgical and medical cases not of an infectious nature, and that the Honorary Medical Officers be authorised to admit proper occupants for the beds."

In the following January the Bolton Chronicle devoted its editorial to the cause with its usual fervour:

BOLTON CHRONICLE 10th January 1852
"THE INFIRMARY AND DISPENSARY
Certainly one of the most deserving institutions in the town is the Infirmary and Dispensary. Besides the purely charitable nature of its operation it affords its assistance at almost the extremity of human need. Just when the power of applying resources is taken away and sickness renders the poor man trebly poor, or when some untoward casualty rots the will of its direction and strikes the body to the ground, crushed, torn, bleeding and helpless, the

Committee step forward to soothe and assist the sufferer, by the most valuable of all aid, that which restores to health and usefulness; and the Institution vindicates its claim to universal support by giving shelter, succour and scientific help to the wounded and afflicted.

It was with no ordinary pleasure, therefore, that we observed a short time since, the movement among those of wealth and influence in the Borough to increasing the means and extending the services of this admirable establishment. A meeting was held, a series of the strongest possible reasons were advanced for the alterations proposed, a Committee was appointed to obtain the necessary subscriptions, and it was unanimously considered that a more desirable object for the town and neighbourhood than that which was contemplated, it was scarcely possible to accomplish. In common, we believe, with a considerable number of inhabitants of Bolton who would be most willing to further the views of the Committee, we have been anxiously awaiting for some evidence that the general success of the Committee's labours has been commensurate with the merits of their appeal, and the extent of their exertions.

So far as our information goes we regret extremely to find that the Committee have been enabled to advance but a comparatively small way towards the accomplishment of their designs. But it is difficult to conceive that with so strong a case for the exercise of humane and benevolent feelings of those addressed, the proceedings of the Committee should be conclusively unsatisfactory, we entertain the strongest hope both that the gentlemen who have taken this matter in hand will be induced to persevere energetically in their good work, and that they will receive a response from our fellow townsmen as will enable them to carry out their eminently philanthropic intentions, and place the Borough at least on a level in this respect with other neighbouring towns of less wealth and smaller numbers. With the view of re-calling attention to this subject in the most prominent manner at our disposal, and giving some assistance to the further labours of the Committee, we gladly insert in this place the following timely and sensible letter from a "working man". There will be found in it facts which deserve the most serious consideration of everyone possessing the ordinary feelings of humanity and which, at a season like the present, should appeal with double force to the Christian and the charitable.

Sir,

On Wednesday the 19th November last a public meeting was held "for the purpose of taking into consideration the propriety of extending the operations of the Bolton Infirmary and Dispensary, by the reception of an increased number of in-patients". At this meeting it was demonstrated that a great necessity existed for such extension; that in consequence of the increase in population, there was a much larger number of serious accidents occurring, and also disorders of a character which could not be successfully treated at the houses of the poor; that the Manchester Infirmary which used to receive inmates from Bolton and neighbourhood was so full that it could not receive one case out of six which it was proposed to send; that instances had occurred of patients being sent to Manchester who had been sent back (and if I am not mistaken I recollect some time since, where a man who had met with a serious accident died, there being an almost certainty that his death was attributable to removal to Manchester); that many gentlemen who subscribed to the Manchester Infirmary were willing to transfer their subscriptions to Bolton, provided adequate accommodation was provided; and that the amount of money raised in Bolton for the support of the Infirmary and Dispensary was much more below the average of towns similarly situated, Stockport being particularly pointed out as, with a smaller population, yearly devoting £756 to Bolton's £377.

In view of these facts, which appear to have had an irresistible effect upon the minds of the gentlemen present, it was resolved that a general canvas for subscriptions should immediately take place. It is now more than six weeks since the meeting was held at which this worthy resolve was come to, and I regret to say that it has not yet been responded to in a manner creditable to the liberality and humanity of my fellow townsmen. Of course, I take it for granted that the resolution for a general canvas has been by the Committee industriously carried out; for if it had not then indeed the limited success may easily be accounted for. Whether that be so or not I shall not stop to enquire, but trust that all will combine to supply a want in the Borough which has neither relation to sect nor party, but is one of suffering humanity. Amongst the names of the gentlemen who have responded to the call of the Committee, I observe one for a munificent donation, which I am glad to see, not merely on account of the largeness of the amount as from the fact that the donor's station (Dr. Chadwick) in society constitutes him one of the very best judges of the necessity of such an institution as the one whose claims I am endeavouring to advocate, and is also a guarantee that the support which is already accorded to it is judiciously distributed. I trust, Sir, that your readers will seriously take this matter into consideration. The sum desired to be raised is of insignificant amount, and can readily be obtained by a united effort. Let none suppose that, disregarding the ordinary dictates of humanity and the calls of Christianity, they are safe, and have no need to take heed as to the condition of the less fortunate members of society, for be it observed contagion is no respecter of persons, and fevers originating in the localities of the poor, which, if the sufferers had been removed to a place where suitable treatment could be applied, might have been extirpated, not unfrequently spread and carry sickness and death into the habitations of the wealthy.

Afraid of unduly trespassing upon your space, I will conclude by a request (with which I should not have troubled you had I, as I have been for some time expecting, been waited upon by some person deputed by the Committee) that you will hand over the enclosed 2s.6d. to the Treasurer of the Institution. I regret the amount is not larger, but it is as great as the claims of a wife and half-a-dozen children will permit out of the earnings of
'A working man'."

The annual meeting in March 1853 indicated that the cries had not gone unheeded and progress had been made. 1,475 ordinary patients had been admitted against the 1,151 of 1851, and the number of Infirmary patients had risen from 24 to 46.

Many Doctors were committed to research and experiement in the treatment of disease, and to its cause. Innumerable 'papers' were presented containing their findings, supported by conclusive evidence. A Dr. Snow provided such evidence that Cholera was spread by contaminated drinking water, and not, as generally accepted, by airborne germs generated in the piles of dung and refuse left rotting in the streets. Florence Nightingale, remembered mainly for her work in the Crimea, had to fight for many years to gain acceptance of the training and provision of fully qualified nursing staff, as a necessity to the recovery of hospital patients. The adage that 'cleanliness is next to Godliness' had not become part of medical practice, Joseph Lister and antiseptic surgery was destined for the late 1860's. Diagnosis was not considered a necessary and precise science; fever, whether it be typhoid, typhus, gastric, etc., was termed 'typhus' and treated as such. Scarlet fever and diptheria were named 'putrid throat'. That 'correct diagnosis is the first requirement in the treatment of the sick' was never seriously considered. Old habits, old treatments, died hard. In 1853 a certain Dr. Jabez Hogg MRCS wrote a Domestic and Surgical Guide for use in the home, and its contents seemed to be more in line with a medieval back-cloth, than in the increasing enlightenment of the 1850's.

Extract of Henbane was recommended for the 'irritations of the kidney and bladder', and Hemlock for cancer, rheumatism

Medicine

The Infirmary and Dispensary (*Bolton Almanac*)

and nervous afflictions. He does point out the possible need of a stomach pump in case of poisoning, though it is hardly likely that such an instrument was standard equipment in homes and cottages. If by accident you lost a finger or toe, it was recommended that it be replaced at once, and kept in position by a plaster made of silk or calico spread with melted resin and soap. It was claimed that even a nose that had been cut from the face was successfully re-jointed by using this method. Leeches were still the answer to inflamed joints, and for diabetes, plenty of meat, castor oil, and a good dose of opium at night was the sure remedy.

Another book appeared in 1853, "The Practice of Medicine on Thomsonian Principles Adapted as well to the use of Families as to that of Practitioners", and based on the work of an American, Dr. Samuel Thomson, Philosopher in Medicine. His philosophy was based on the simple principle that "heat is life, and cold is death". His treatment for all diseases from Ague to Ulcers centred around vapour baths and tincture of lobelia. Hot drinks made with cayenne pepper were also of some help. To his credit he did strongly condemn 'bloodletting', as more likely to kill the patient rather than cure, and insisted that "bloodletting will not always relieve pain, except the patient be brought so low by it as to destroy his sensibility."

Despite reaction against change and reform, medical practice, like all other forms of social welfare, was beginning to accept new principles and their application, albeit at a snail-like pace, and some benefit was reaching those who were most in need.

WAR

The end of Napoleon and a relatively peaceful Europe had allowed the energies, talents, and convictions of the British nation, backed by the unchallengeable supremacy of the Navy, to penetrate all parts of the globe, in search of commerce and expansion.

With involvement in so many countries it was inevitable that some friction would occur. Insults would have to be avenged, minor insurrections put down, Englishmen who had managed to get themselves involved in some predicament would have to be rescued, and the offender chastised. Consequently the British Army and its native recruits were continually in action. These 'minor' wars and campaigns hardly raised comment in local papers, but Russian aspirations in Turkey were to result in a 'major' confrontation.

The Victorian soldier was an enigma; recruited from the slums, poorly paid, fed, and housed, subjected to brutal discipline, and despised by the public, yet he was imbibed with Regimental pride and tradition, and on active service displayed outstanding qualities and stoicism. Pay for a private soldier was one shilling per day, plus a penny a day beer money, but from this fourpence-halfpenny was deducted for rations, and from the remaining eightpence-halfpenny there were deductions for barrack-room damages, losses and cleaning materials. The coming war in the Crimea was to test his resilience and his ability to survive and fight in abominable conditions.

The declaration of war in March 1854 was the result of the Russians demanding a protectorate in Turkey following an obscure religious quarrel, in the hope that they could take over Constantinople and gain an outlet to the Mediterranean. Britain and the European powers wanted no Russian influence in that sphere. Many Government Ministers and MPs were, in private, against a war, whose causes could have been settled by diplomacy and negotiation, but the populace, encouraged by the newspapers, wanted war. There had been forty years of peace, and it was time for some excitement, time for an opportunity for patriotic fervour and flag-waving, military splendour and parades.

BOLTON CHRONICLE 22nd April 1854
"THE DAY OF HUMILIATION AND FASTING
Whereas our Most Gracious Majesty The Queen having, by her Royal Proclamation commanded that a Public Day of Humiliation and Prayer be observed throughout Great Britain and Ireland on Wednesday, the 26th day of April instant, humbly to supplicate Almighty God and implore His Blessing and Assistance on our Arms both by sea and land for the Restoration of Peace; and strictly charging that the said day be reverently and devoutly observed by all Her Majesty's loving subjects. The Mayor in this publicity notifying Her Majesty's Proclamation, so appropriately issued, feels assured that the inhabitants of Bolton and its neighbourhood will most thankfully and strictly observe the Royal Command, and that all places of business will be closed.
 P. R. Arrowsmith. Mayor.
Bolton 21st April 1854 GOD SAVE THE QUEEN."

The manner in which the war was to be conducted invited catastrophic defeat. Lord Raglan, the appointed Commander-in-Chief, was 66 years of age. He had been A.D.C. to Wellington at Waterloo, where he had lost an arm, and had seen no further action since that day, and had never before commanded an army in the field. The officers and men comprising the army of some 27,000, were drafted from England, and the bulk had no experience of active service, but were more at home on the barrack square. Senior officers who had experience of warfare, particularly in India, for some reason were socially unacceptable, and Lord Raglan would have none of them.

The administration of the Army was as muddled as the army itself, due to the organisation not the individual. Food and transport was provided and maintained by the Commissariat, which was not part of the Army, but was a department of the Treasury; the Medical Department was not responsible to the Commander-in-Chief, but to the Secretary for War; the Secretary of State was not responsible for financing the Royal Artillery and the Royal Engineers, they came under the Master-General of the Ordnance; the size of the Army and its cost was not the responsibility of either the Secretary for War, the Commander-in-Chief, or the Chancellor of the Exchequer, but was directly and solely controlled by the Secretary of State for the Colonies. Organised chaos seems to be the appropriate term.

The army embarked in uniform more suitable to a pageant in high summer; scarlet tunics, shining brass helmets, hussars, lancers, dragoons in glorious technicolour, green jackets and spotless white accoutrements, and cavalry horses groomed to perfection. It was remarked that Lord Cardigan's Hussars in their tight plum coloured pants were more suited to the ballet.

Wealthy officers sailed off in their yachts, wives and their maids insisted on joining the party, and tourists amended their itinerary to follow the army and watch the fun.

Reality was more grim; by the time the army disembarked at Varna, a port on the Black Sea, many of the splendid cavalry horses had perished and the remnants were in poor shape, and dysentery and cholera were spreading among the men.

The British, French and Turkish armies finally invaded the Crimean Peninsular in the middle of September, much later than they had intended to do. The whole strategy of the campaign was to capture and destroy the fortified naval base of Sebastopol, which would effectively end the war. The dilatory nature of both British and French commands allowed the Russians ample time to reinforce the approaches to the objective. The navy was hardly less blameless:

BOLTON CHRONICLE 23rd September 1854
"TO CRONSTADT AND BACK
The Baltic fleet is coming home. At a time when merchant vessels do not think it too late to make a voyage to St. Petersburg, and when our trade with Russia is usually at its highest, that vast and powerful fleet, upon the irresistible strength of which we prided ourselves so highly, when it took its departure from our shores six months ago, and its Commander, from whose experience, daring and skill, such things were anticipated, are returning to England. Cronstadt, Sveaborg, Riga, Revel, stand uninjured; not a hostile shot or shell has been thrown into any of them, not a ship has been taken out of their harbours, and yet we are told the season for active operations is over! Over, why when did it commence? Are sailing to Cronstadt and back and taking a peep at Sveabord from a safe distance, active operations? What then has caused Napier the daring to dare nothing? This is a mystery we cannot unfold."

Before the fleet had sailed a pen-picture of its Commander, Sir Charles Napier had appeared in the Bolton Chronicle.

"A PORTRAIT OF SIR CHARLES NAPIER.
A farmer looking man with a fat face, thick lips, and a tremendous nose covered with snuff, large ears like the flaps of a saddle, and like 'Uncle Ned' in lyric history, with no wool to speak of on top of his head, although his phrenological developments display an extensive surface where the wool ought to grow; the head placed on the body of a stunted alderman, whose clothes appear to have been pitch-forked on his back, with one shirt collar higher than the other, his waistcoat buttoned awry, and his shirt-front smeared with snuff – and you have the portrait of Sir Charles Napier."

Not an exactly flattering picture.

The Russians had occupied the heights of Alma, barring the way to Sebastopol, and on the morning of the 20th September the battle of Alma began.

BOLTON CHRONICLE 7th October 1854
"THE VICTORIES IN THE CRIMEA.
The reception of the news of the splendid success of the Allies on the heights of Alma, and the reported capture of Sebastopol, and partial destruction of the Russian Fleet, produced a profound sensation in this town, and for the time being monopolised all other considerations. The first intimation of the victory of the allied troops in the Crimea was a verbal despatch received on Sunday morning by Mr. Greenhalgh, the Postmaster, stating that Sebastopol had been taken, and this statement was supposed to receive some confirmation from the fact that in the same morning several persons in the vicinity of Rivington heard heavy and continuous firing in the direction of Liverpool, which they believed to be rejoicings for some great victory; of course the news of so important an event was soon known from one end of the town to the other. St. George's Church bells were rung in honour of the occasion. On Monday evening Trinity Church tower was illuminated, flags waved from every pinnacle and many of the principal buildings in the town; guns were fired to commemorate the victory, and everybody seemed satisfied with what they were led to believe was an accomplished fact. On Tuesday evening a band of music, connected with Mr. Bolling's works, paraded the principal streets carrying torchlights, banners and a ludicrous effigy of 'old Menshikov'. Last night again the fifes and drums, guided on their way by one solitary torchlight, perambulated the town, and in front of the procession of ragged boys and girls, was

borne a huge banner on which was inscribed "Capture of Sebastopol"."

The Chronicle's cautious approach to the report was justified, and a later paragraph confirmed this –

"After all Sebastopol is not fallen. It is now supposed that the accounts which were published earlier in the week, in which all the circumstances connected with the supposed capture of Sebastopol were minutely detailed, were neither more or less than stock-jobbing figments. It is a monstrous scandal that money making men, men who stand high in the commercial world, men against whose private character no one could venture to breathe a word of scandal, should be thus capable of inventing the most horrible lies for the purpose of imposing upon the silly dupe- the public. We do not remember any occasion in the history of this country in which probability has been so completely outraged as in the recent fabricated accounts of the fall of Sebastopol."

A further paragraph was to follow:

"*GREAT VICTORY OVER THE RUSSIANS*
Authentic intelligence has been received of a sanguinary engagement having been taken place between the allies and the Russians on the heights of Alma, near Sebastopol, resulting in the defeat and immense slaughter of the Russian forces, and we have unhappily to add, with the loss of nearly three thousand lives on the part of English and French.

Lord Raglan states that the entrenchments at Alma were carried an hour-and-a-half after sunset. The enemy fought with desperation. Nothing could exceed the bravery and excellent conduct of the troops. The Russian position was very formidable and defended by guns of heavy calibre. A few Russian prisoners were taken among whom were two general officers."

There was the usual muddle and indecision after the battle, and the remnants of the Russian army were allowed to retreat unharassed to Sebastopol, and given time to reinforce the already formidable defences.

The tiny harbour of Balaclava was selected by the allies as their supply base, and it was from here that the first ominous reports began to be sent home by William Russell, The Times correspondent in the Crimea.

"During the first three weeks of our stay in the Crimea we lost as many of cholera as perished on the Alma (about two thousand British). The town (Balaclava) was in a filthy revolting state. Lord Raglan ordered it to be cleansed, but there was no one to obey the order, and consequently no one attended to it."

On 25th October the Russians left their Sebastopol fortress and attacked in superior numbers to capture Balaclava. They completely overwhelmed the Turks manning the first line of defence. A triumphant stand was made by the Highland Regiment, who broke the full weight of the Russian Cavalry charge. Russell wrote of "that thin red streak tipped with a line of steel". The Heavy Cavalry Brigade took on more than twice its number of élite Russian Cavalry. Russell again sent home an eloquent despatch –

"As lightning flashed through cloud, the Greys and Enniskilleners pierced through the masses of Russians. The shock was but for a moment. There was a clash of steel and a light play of sword-blades in the air, and then the Greys and the redcoats disappeared in the midst of the shaken and quivering columns. In another moment we saw them emerging with diminished numbers and in broken order, charging against the second line. It was a terrible moment. The first line of Russians which had been utterly smashed by our charge, and had fled off at one flank and towards the centre, were coming back to swallow up our handful of men. By sheer steel and sheer courage Enniskillener and Scot were winning their desperate way right through the enemy's squadrons, and already grey horses and red coats had appeared right at the rear of the second mass, when, with irresistible force, like one bolt from a bow, the 4th Dragoon Guards riding straight at the right flank of the Russians, and the 5th Dragoon Guards, following close after the Enniskilleners, rushed at the remnants of the first line of the enemy, went through it as though it were made of pasteboard and put them to utter rout."

This was the sort of "adventure" story that the country and Bolton were anxious to read in their newspapers. That appetite was appeased even more by the episode which followed next:

BOLTON CHRONICLE 18th November 1854
"BALACLAVA – THE CAVALRY CATASTROPHE
And now occurred the melancholy catastrophe which fills us all with sorrow. It appears that the Quartermaster General Brigadier Airey, thinking that the Light Cavalry had not gone far enough in front when the enemy's horse had fled, gave an order in writing to Captain Nolan, 15th Hussars, to take to Lord Lucan directing his

Lordship "to advance his cavalry nearer to the enemy". A braver soldier than Captain Nolan the army did not possess. He was known to all his arm of the service for his entire devotion to his profession, and his name most familiar to all who take interest in our cavalry, for his excellent work published a year ago on our system of drill and remount, and breaking horses. When Lord Lucan received the order from Captain Nolan and had read it, he asked "where are we to advance to". Captain Nolan pointed his finger to the line of Russians and said "There are the enemy and there are the guns, Sir, before them, it is your duty to take them". Lord Lucan, with reluctance gave the order to Lord Cardigan to advance upon the guns, conceiving that his orders compelled him to do so. The noble Earl, though he did not shrink, also saw the fearful odds against him. Don Quixote in his tilt against the windmills, was not near so rash and reckless as the gallant fellows who prepared without a thought to rush to almost certain death.

They advanced in two lines quickening their pace as they closed towards the enemy, a more fearful spectacle was never witnessed than those who, without the power to aid, beheld their heroic countrymen rushing into the arms of death. At the distance of 1200 yards the whole line of the enemy belched forth from thirty iron mouths a flood of smoke and flame through which hissed the deadly balls. The flight was marked by instant gaps in our ranks, by dead men and horses, by steeds flying wounded or riderless across the plain. The first line is broken, it is joined by the second, they never halt or check their speed an instant; with diminished ranks, thinned by those thirty guns, with a halo of flashing steel above their heads, and with a cheer which was many a noble fellow's death cry, they flew into the smoke of the batteries. Through the clouds of smoke we could see their sabres flashing as they rode up to the guns and dashed between them, cutting down the gunners as they stood. At 11.35 not a British Soldier was left in front of those bloody Muscovie guns. Our loss, as far as it could be ascertained in killed, wounded and missing at two o-clock was as follows:-

	Went into Action	Returned from Action	Loss
4th Light Dragoons	118	39	79
8th Hussars	104	38	66
11th Hussars	110	25	85
13th Lancers	130	61	69
17th Lancers	145	35	110

The battle ended with the Russians back in Sebastopol, the British and French retaining their supply base at Balaclava, a lot of killed and wounded, and a large enough measure of deeds of daring and glory to satisfy the newspapers and the avid readers back in Britain.

Having failed with massed cavalry to take Balaclava, the Russians on 5th November launched an attack with 40,000 foot soldiers on the British positions. The concerted efforts of the infantry and cavalry forced Menshikov to retreat back to Sebastopol. This battle of Inkerman cost the Russians 12,000 casualties. The British had lost 3,300. Two days later Russell toured the battlefield, and ended his despatch to The Times with –

> "If it is considered that the soldiers who met these furious columns of the Czar were the remnants of three British Divisions, which scarcely numbered 8,500 men, that they were hungry and wet and half-famished; that they were men belonging to a force which was generally 'out of bed' four nights out of seven; which had been enfeebled by sickness, by severe toil, sometimes for twenty-four hours at a time without relief of any kind; that among them were men who had within a short time previously lain out for forty-eight hours in the trenches at a stretch – it will be readily admitted that never was a more extraordinary contest maintained by our army since it acquired a reputation in the world's history."

The concern which Russell was increasingly showing in his despatches, was justified. The enemy was safely entrenched in Sebastopol, able to reinforce and supply the garrison without hindrance; the British were occupying open positions around Balaclava, which was proving to be an inadequate base. The whole supply position was in chaos, and to add to the problems a hurricane on 14th November sank nearly thirty supply ships, with the loss of food, clothing and medical supplies. The badly depleted British Divisions were in no condition to mount any attack on the Russian fortress, and they were faced with contending with the ever increasing severity of winter weather. A sergeant of the Royal Fusiliers wrote in his narrative of the campaign –

> "– all was higgledy-piggledy and confusion. The cavalry horses, that had cost an enormous amount, sank up to their knees in mud at every step until they dropped exhausted; and all the way from the camp to Balaclava were to be seen dead horses, mules and bullocks, in every stage of decomposition. And our poor fellows – who had fought so well at the Alma, Balaclava and the two Inkermans – were

now dying by hundreds daily. The army was put upon half rations – half a pound of mouldy biscuit and half a pound of salt junk (pork or beef); coffee was served out, but in its raw, green state, with no means of roasting it. No wood or firing was to be had, except a few roots that were dug up. The whole camp was one vast sheet of mud, the trenches in many places knee deep; men died at their posts from sheer exhaustion or starvation rather than complain, for if they reported themselves sick the medical chests were empty."

The sick and the wounded had to be transported for three hundred miles by boat across the Black Sea to the inadequate base hospital at Scutari. The horrific conditions described in despatches and letters were beginning to rouse some attention, and one outcome was the sending of Florence Nightingale and a staff of thirty-eight nurses to attempt some improvement. They arrived at Scutari in time to deal with the casualties from the battle of Balaclava and a further six hundred wounded from the Battle of Inkerman.

What had started as a picnic was now being seen as something entirely different. Comment in the Bolton Chronicle read –

"It is now established, to use General Evan's words, that we entered upon the war as if there were to be no wounds, no necessity for magazines of ammunition, food or stores."

It was also realised that not all casualties were in the Crimea; the high death roll left many widows and orphans in great need –

BOLTON CHRONICLE 14th October 1854
"THE WIDOWS AND ORPHANS OF OUR SOLDIERS.
We find that movements have been initiated in neighbouring towns for the purpose of raising subscriptions among the working classes towards maintaining the widows and orphans of those brave fellows who have perished during the present war in the Crimea, and who have fallen victims to the pestilence whilst languishing in the dismal climate of Varna.

If the operatives, artisans and mechanics of all classes would unite a very considerable sum might be raised in the town by small weekly subscriptions of a half-penny or a penny from each person. If there are 12,000 persons in Bolton capable of sparing a penny a week, and we are assured that there are so many, it would amount to £500 in ten weeks. Carry out the same principle through all the large towns in the Kingdom, and it will be found that so trivial a sacrifice as a penny a week from the wages of working people of this country for the same time would more than suffice to provide an asylum and the means of subsistence to all the widows and orphans whom the events of the present war may cast upon the nation. But we do not mean that the 'operative' classes alone should be called upon to contribute towards so praiseworthy an object. We only mention them first because they have greater facilities for uniting in so benevolent a scheme. The middle classes and the higher classes have already nobly contributed and we have no doubt that they will do so again when called upon. The soldier's widow and children should be looked upon as the nation's property, or rather as having an irresistible claim upon the nation for support. This principle is distinctly recognised in the case of those who have been wounded in battle, they are pensioned for life at the expense of the nation. Why should not the poor widows and orphans have a similar provision, at least a voluntary one, if not included in the estimates.

Sure we are that our Bolton operatives will feel proud to have an opportunity of assuaging the sorrows of those who have been bereaved by the present righteous war."

BOLTON CHRONICLE 2nd December 1854
"THE PATRIOTIC FUND
Right nobly, indeed, have our townsmen and neighbours responded to the call which has been made to them on behalf of the Patriotic Fund. It is only a few days since the first appeal was put forth on account of this national and truly philanthropic object, and already the subscription list embraces an aggregate sum of about £500. This is extremely gratifying, and it shows that the hearts of the people of Bolton are fairly and fully enlisted in this benevolent exercise. The spontaneous and self-denying efforts of the working classes demand our special commendation, long may they be blessed in the grateful prayers of the widows and orphans of the brave defenders of our national honour."

The progress of the war, or the lack of it, caused a further Royal appeal for a day of fast and prayer –

BOLTON CHRONICLE 24th March 1855
"THE NATIONAL FAST
Wednesday last being the day appointed by proclamation for a solemn fast, humiliation and prayer before Almighty God in order (as set forth in the Royal Decree) to obtain pardon for our sins, and in the most devout and solemn manner send up our prayers and supplications to the Divine Majesty imploring His Blessing, and assistance on our arms for the restoration of peace to Her Majesty and her Dominions. Religious services were celebrated in the various churches of the establishment, and in most of the dissenting and other places of worship in this town and neighbourhood. With few exceptions the mills and workshops

were closed, most of the tradesmen's shops were also closed, and there was a very general observation of the day, so far as the suspension of business was concerned. The congregations at most of the places of worship were large, and were evidently impressed with the solemnity of the object for which they were assembled.

The unusual fineness of the weather, however, induced many people to take advantage of the holiday for a ramble in the country, and more than one snug little picnic party betook themselves to Rivington and the neighbouring hills, thinking, no doubt, (whether right or wrong we are not here called upon to say) that the body corporal would derive greater benefit from inhaling the invigorating breezes of the hilly region, and the requirements of the inner man be better satisfied by a hearty lunch, than by any compliance with the requirements of our Church by observing the day as one of 'fasting' in the strict acceptance of that term."

The reports from the Crimea did produce quick government action and a Committee of Enquiry was set up, and the Committee itself did proceed with commendable speed, and was able to present its findings to Parliament on 18th June 1855 –

"MR. ROEBUCK'S COMMITTEE OF ENQUIRY
PRESENTED BEFORE THE HOUSE OF COMMONS ON MONDAY, 18th June 1855
EXTRACTS
From the middle of November this army was during a period of many weeks reduced to a condition which it is melancholy to contemplate, but which was endured both by officers and men with a fortitude and heroism unsurpassed in the annals of war. They were exposed under single canvas to all the sufferings and inconveniences of cold, rain, mud and snow, on high ground, and in the depth of winter. They suffered from overwork, exposure, want of clothing, insufficient supplies for the healthy and imperfect accommodation for the sick.

Encamped in a hostile country at a distance of 3,000 miles from England, and engaged during a severe winter in besieging a fortress which, from want of numbers, it could not invest, it was necessarily placed in a situation where unremitting fatigue and hardship had to be endured. Your Committee are, however, of opinion that this amount of unavoidable suffering had been aggravated by causes hereafter enumerated, and which are mainly to be attributed to dilatory and insufficient arrangements for the supply of this army with the necessaries indispensable to its healthy and effective condition.

The administration which ordered the expedition had no adequate information as to the amount of the forces in the Crimea.

They were not acquainted with the strength of the fortresses to be attacked, or with the resources of the country to be invaded. They hoped and expected the expedition to be immediately successful, and as they did not foresee the probability of a protracted struggle, they made no provision for a winter campaign. Your Committee, in conclusion, cannot but remark that the first real improvements in the lamentable condition of hospitals at Scutari are to be attributed to private suggestions, private exertions, and private benevolence."

The Bolton Chronicle remarked –

"Well might the 'Peelites' resign rather than sanction such an enquiry as that which has resulted in the report before us. We cannot, and do not, believe that any British Statesman is traitorous to his country, but we do say, if the men who blindly sent the British Army to the Crimea, and left it to rot there, had been in the pay of Russia, they could not more effectually have done the work of the enemy."

By the Spring of 1855, the combined outcry of Russell's despatches, public opinion, and Roebuck's Court of Enquiry report, had resulted in a flurry of activity, and a flow of reinforcements and supplies had arrived in the Crimea. Through May to September more determination was shown in containing the Russians in Sebastopol, and on the 8th September desperate attacks were made on the key fortresses of Malakoff and the Redan. French troops captured their objective, the Redan, but the British took but could not hold Malakoff. Despite this set-back the Russians had had enough, and the following day blew up the remaining forts and destroyed everything else in the town that they could before abandoning the place.

BOLTON CHRONICLE 29th September 1855
"FALL OF SEBASTOPOL
The principal stores were destroyed, the town was set on fire, the forts were partially blown up, the bridge of boats removed, and the vessels in the harbour sunk, in the course of the retreat to the northern fortifications. The Allied forces, as well may be imagined, entered the town with very great caution. The scene that presented itself on both sides of the inner harbour was most appalling. The bombardment had produced the most fearful effects. What was, twelve months ago, a stately city, full of costly public works is now

a shapeless mass of blackened ruins, stained with human blood, and reeking with corruption.
DAYS OF THANKSGIVING
Tomorrow (30th September) has been set apart for the solemn observance of a "day of prayer and thanksgiving for the signal and repeated successes obtained by the troops of Her Majesty and by those of Her Allies in the Crimea, and especially for the capture of Sebastopol." "

Both the Russians and the Allies had no inclination to continue the fight, and peace negotiations resulted in the signing of a treaty in Paris in April 1856 –

BOLTON CHRONICLE 5th April 1856
"RECEPTION OF THE PEACE NEWS IN BOLTON
Intelligence of the signature of the treaty of peace by the plenipotentiaries at Paris was received in this town at an early hour on Monday morning, and soon became generally known.

There were few parties to whom the news was not a source of satisfaction; some hailed it with unbounded manifestations of delight, rubbed their hands in gleeful anticipation of brightening prospects, and strode through the streets as the "good time coming" so long foretold had at last actually made an appearance. There were others, however, who were not disposed to take so cheerful a view of the matter, who were not quite satisfied that England had not lost some laurels in this war, and who thought that another campaign would have redeemed past blunders and won back for us that ancient prestige, which had made us the envy and admiration of surrounding nations. But most people took a more sober view of it, and congratulated each other on the termination of a strife which had occasioned so much bloodshed, and the day being remarkably fine, not a few converted it into a holiday. Particulars of the signature of the treaty were printed at the Chronicle office early in the morning and some hundreds of slips given away. Flags were soon hoisted upon the various churches, the Post Office, the mills and foundries, and principal buildings of the town; and a considerable number were hung out from the shops in Deansgate, Churchgate, Bradshawgate, Bridge Street and Bank Street. The Church bells rang forth merry peals, and an air of rejoicing manifested itself on all sides, though the news of peace was not hailed with that intense enthusiasm which greeted the fall of Sebastopol.

A general illumination was suggested, but met no encouragement, and the only demonstration we noted of this kind was one in the form of a star in front of Mr. Telfor's Fleece Inn, Bradshawgate."

THE INDIAN MUTINY

The Crimean War had tarnished the image of the might of British arms, but the worst was still to come.

The East India Company 'ruled' India, not the Crown; the Indian Army belonged to them. There were a few British Regiments, but the bulk of the armed forces were regiments of native troops, commanded and led by British officers. The incident of the cartridges greased with pig and cow fat which caused the first shots to be fired, was the culmination of growing discontent among the sepoys, a discontent that was fanned by religious fanatics and disgruntled princes.

Neither the East India Company administrators nor the representatives of the Crown, could comprehend that the 'natives' might not accept that the British concept of justice, morality and religion was the only way of life. It was beyond their powers to appreciate the importance of caste, of Muslim and Hindu customs and ceremony, so it was not difficult for the agitators to convince their people, including the sepoys, that their culture was threatened. There had been a great influx of missionaries into India, who tackled the work of converting the heathen with great fervour, which again lent credence to the rumours that the British intended to force the Hindus and Muslims to forsake their religions for Christianity.

It was in this climate that the sepoys at Meerut rebelled against the command to 'bite' the cartridges which they thought were contaminated with animal fat, and so started the great Mutiny.

The Mutiny began on 10th May 1857, but it was weeks later before the first news reached London. On 4th July the Bolton Chronicle published in full the despatch from The Times correspondent in Bombay, written on 27th May.

> "In my letter of the 11th I mentioned that a telegraphic message had that afternoon arrived at Bombay from Agra to the effect that the 3rd Bengal Light Cavalry, stationed at Meerut, was in a state of open mutiny. The report soon received ample confirmation, and worse was to follow. For several days the intelligence from the North West told of nothing but revolt and murder. As was expected much thus reported has since turned out to be untrue. Stations said to be disturbed are found to be perfectly quiet, and eminent public servants asserted to have fallen victims to the soldier are preserved to their families and to the State."

The Times correspondent closed his detailed report by observing –

"Would that we had a dozen more English regiments. Pity that the "Himalaya", the "Retribution", the "Transit" and the rest are not bound for the Sandheads instead of Hong Kong. The quarrel with the lethargic Chinaman might keep – not so that with the explosive Bengal sepoy."

There had been mutiny before in India, but these had remained localised and been quickly and mercilessly crushed, so that no great concern was given to yet another native rebellion. The Bolton Chronicle, in its leader column, on 4th July, did think fit to comment on the whole system of governing India, and considered in many ways that the mutiny was a blessing in disguise.

". . . representing, as we do, a community as English in spirit, and patriotic in feeling as any in the kingdom, we trust we run no risk of being misunderstood when we say that it is a long time since news arrived from India, for which we felt more disposed to be thankful than that which arrived last week. Never till now did we feel a perfect assurance that to England, for as many centuries as God's high purposes require, the dominion of India is secured. Hitherto our empire there, in its extent, its richness, the rapidity with which it was acquired, and the precarious tenure by which we held it, had a character of unsubstantiality about it which made it resemble more a dream than reality.

A dominion maintained by some 40,000 Europeans over 160,000,000 of natives, whom they themselves, and the march of time, and the diffusion of ideas, were training in the arts of war and peace, inoculating with European ideas, and making participations of English liberties, could not have lasted, and – we may admit the fact now that the system is doomed – ought not to have lasted. Supposing neither the Mussulman nor the Hindu ever to have acquired the courage and force to expel us, by slow degrees the Russian or the Yankee would have pushed forward their intrigues and their entrenchments, and wrested from us the empire of which we have proved ourselves unworthy. And talking of Russia, are we are not bound at all events to acknowledge with thankfulness, the narrow escape we have had? This mutiny, by the accounts we have had of it, is a serious matter enough in itself, and the Government have shown their sense of the danger, by ordering with unexampled rapidity for them, the instant embarkation of 14,000 men, in addition to the troops intercepted on their route from

Persia to China. But what if it had occurred while we were at war with Russia, and our troops engaged at Sebastopol or in Asia Minor? We have no doubt that Russia meant it to be so. We have not a shadow of doubt that the Persian War, and the Chinese War, and now this Indian insurrection, are all of them trains which Russia laid two or three years ago, but which have only now exploded. Had the war continued and Russia succeeded in effecting this treble diversion in the strongholds of our Asiatic dominion and prestige, what would have become of us? Our people are brave and our wealth unparalleled, but what bravery and what resources could have availed to carry on a Russian and a Persian, and an Indian and a Chinese war all at the same time? To save ourselves in one quarter we must have let go the others, and so yield the prestige of the present and the vantage ground of the future to our subtle and intriguing foe. God ordered it otherwise; and so we find out in the very day and hour that His chastising hand is upon us.

By the light of the lesser calamity we read the story of the greater one, which in His mercy He withheld."

The Chronicle had its own recipe for success –

"The only reliable safeguard against the Indians, and against the Russians, and against the Afghans, and against the Nepaulese, now and for all time, is extensive colonization by British and other Europeans, of the more temperate parts of India. Let our 40,000 or 80,000 European soldiers and civilians have a reserve to fall back upon say of 4,000,000 or 8,000,000 European colonists on the slopes of the Himalayas. Let India, like America, have her millions of inhabitants of European descent, and then, and then only, will the resources of the glorious region be developed, and the natives rescued from their present state of penury, apathy and status quo, into the worthy and profitable subjects of the mighty empire of which they form so large a part."

On 18th July a supplement to the Bolton Chronicle was published largely concerned with news from India. 36 native regiments were listed as mutinied or disbanded, but the abstract from the "Observer" still claimed "it will probably not turn out to be so alarming as it looks."

On 8th August the Bolton Chronicle was listing 78 Native Regiments mutinied or disbanded. Lists of missing persons were now being published and accounts of atrocities were being received from numerous garrison towns, not only from official despatches, but from private letters reaching England. By 29th

August the Bolton Chronicle was joining in the growing chorus for swift and terrible vengeance.

> "We cannot think of reproducing the worst of these horrors, still least of defiling our leading columns with them, but all who have read the bulk of the letters recently published will be sufficiently aware of what we allude to. The defilements inflicted on hundreds of delicate women and innocent children for days together, often in the presence of their husbands and fathers, terminated by brutal exposure and piecemeal mutilation, when ever refinement of malignity had been exhausted. Fathers, husbands, brothers of England, think of it, and give up yourselves for retribution. If ever there was a cause that called for instant and unmitigated punishment, it is this. If ever human blood cried to the Lord for vengeance, it is this. If 100,000 or 200,000 men were needed to crush for ever the cowardly wretches who have thus repaid the most lenient rule ever wielded by a dominant race, you ought not to grudge them. Every village in the land ought to send forth its contingent of volunteers in such a cause. The whole resources of the Empire ought to be put forth to vindicate the right and the might of England, thoroughly to avenge her children and wipe from the annals of the human race, so far as condign punishment can do, the stigma of enormities so hideous, so fiendishly base, and filthy as to be all but incredible."

BOLTON CHRONICLE 12th September 1857
"RELIEF FOR THE SUFFERERS IN INDIA
The harrowing details which continue to reach this country from the scenes of the Indian mutinies are calculated to excite our warmest sympathies. The great amount of suffering which our countrymen and countrywomen have had to endure can scarcely be imagined by the bulk of our own population. We can form but a faint idea of the terrors and privations to which they have been subjected, but faint as our conceptions of these horrible scenes are they are sufficient to awaken in the public mind a generous desire to lend the assistance of British charity at the desperate crisis which has visited our Indian Empire. The metropolis has already been the scene of active exertions to alleviate the more pressing wants and trials of those who have been robbed of their all on the plains and in the blood stained towns and fortresses of Hindoostan; and other large towns are following the generous impulse which initiated the noble subscriptions in London. We trust that Bolton will emulate so worthy an example, and that the Mayor and clergy and other authorities will come forward, willingly, actively, and promptly, to aid in so humane an undertaking. The sooner the movement in this

matter takes place the better, as the wants to be relieved are most urgent."
BOLTON CHRONICLE 3rd October 1857
"NOTICE CONVENED BY THE MAYOR
I hereby convene a Public Meeting of the inhabitants of Bolton to be holden at the Town Hall, Little Bolton, on Monday next, 5th October instant, at seven o-clock in the evening, in order that an opportunity may be presented for them to express their sympathy with the cruel sufferings of our countrymen and countrywomen in India, and for the purpose of organising means for raising subscriptions for their relief, consequent upon the atrocious and unheard of calamities to which they have been and are subjected, in that distant part of the British Empire."

Sympathy was such that by November 28th the people of Bolton had donated £1470.11s.5½d. to the Indian Relief Fund.

Delhi, Cawnpore, Lucknow, became household names, and a tide of emotion swept the country, crying for vengeance. The terrible justice of the God of Abraham was invoked; fire and sword was demanded to cleanse that part of the Empire which had made bloody rebellion, and had dared question the righteousness and benevolence of British rule.

The avenging forces answered in full; the scenes at Cawnpore in particular inflamed both officers and men, retribution was brutal, innocent suffered with the guilty, and communities suspected of harbouring rebels were utterly destroyed.

At no time had the uprising involved the greater part of the Indian population; had it been so that vast population would have swept the British out of the continent. The rebel forces still far outnumbered the British troops and loyal sepoys; the mutinous sepoys were well trained and well armed, as were the private armies of the rebellious Indian Princes, but they were hampered by the indisciplined rabble that swelled their ranks, and, most of all, by lack of leadership. The Commanders of the British forces were a different breed than the incompetent staff of the shambles in the Crimea, and led with a skill and daring which shattered the overwhelming superiority of the rebels.

The full suppression of the mutiny was not completed until the end of 1859. It did result in the East India Company losing its privileged control of India, and subsequently Victoria was proclaimed Empress. India became the 'brightest jewel in the Imperial Crown'.

ODD ITEMS

BOLTON CHRONICLE 20th July 1850
"TERRIFIC THUNDERSTORMS
Such an extensive and formidable thunderstorm as seldom occurs in Lancashire visited a considerable portion of the county on Tuesday last, when uncommonly large floods of water fell in repeated torrents, and an immense amount of electricity was discharged from the clouds. The effects, as will be seen from the accompanying intelligence, were sadly deplorable, a number of lives having been taken away and serious havoc done to property. Mr. Ralph Shaw, Farmer, of Lostock, has suffered the loss of a foal worth £10, which was killed in a field, and he is a further loser of £20 by a quantity of hay being flooded.

Mr. James Latham, Farmer, of Lostock had a three year old colt worth £30 and a draught horse valued at £20, both of which were killed in a field.

At the farm of Mr. John Warburton in Lostock, three acres of mown grass and five acres of unmown grass was spoiled by being flooded. Mr. Warburton's loss is estimated at £60."

BOLTON CHRONICLE 28th September 1850
"EMIGRATION TO AUSTRALIA
NEW LINE OF PACKETS FROM LIVERPOOL
REDUCED FARES   —   1st Cabin   —   £45
                     2nd Cabin   —   £25
                     Intermediate   —   £15
                     Steerage   —   £10
ACCOMMODATION SECOND TO NONE
PETREL   1,300 tons to sail 10th October
CONDOR   1,500 tons to sail 10th December
OSPREY   1,200 tons to sail 10th February

BOLTON CHRONICLE 24th September 1853
"GOLD REGIONS OF AUSTRALIA YA
HOME FOR THE EMIGRANT
LAMBERT'S Patent ventilated Double and Single Roofed

AUSTRALIAN TENTS, divided into private apartments for convenience of families or parties. The roof forming a second floor for stowing away goods, etc. The only complete canvas house yet invented, and thoroughly impervious to wet. May be had on application to the Patentee –
R. Lambert, George's Dock, Liverpool.
Lambert's registered GOLD-SIFTER, Emigrants IRON FOLDING CHAIRS and BEDSTEADS in every variety. BEDS, BLANKETS, RUGS, PORTABLE COOKING KITCHENS, TOOLS, and every article required by the emigrant."

BOLTON CHRONICLE 21st April 1853
"The number of various vehicles which passed through Crown Street between the hours of 6 am to 8 pm was:-

Waggons	–	104
Carts	–	900
Donkey Carts	–	94
Cabs & Carriages	–	92
Gigs	–	32
Handcarts & Wheelbarrows	–	128
Horses	–	65"

BOLTON CHRONICLE 12th February 1854
"DECIMAL CURRENCY – MEETING OF THE TOWN COUNCIL
The following petition was adopted on the motion of Mr. Thomasson –
To The Honourable the Commons of the United Kingdom of Great Britain and Ireland in Parliament assembled.
The humble petition of the Mayor, Aldermen and Burgesses of the Borough of Bolton, under their Common Seal, sheweth – That they have seen with great satisfaction the report of a Committee of your honourable House, generally known as the Decimal Coinage Committee, and most fully concur in the plan it has suggested and recommended for the establishment of a system of a decimal coinage, the simplicity of which over that now in use, your petitioners believe would be of great advantage in abridging the time now necessary for the instruction of youth in the knowledge of arithmetic, and would be of great service in facilitating the commercial operations of the Country. Your petitioners therefore humbly pray that your honourable House will lose no time in passing a law for the establishment of such a system, and your petitioners will ever pray."

Odd Items

BOLTON CHRONICLE 4th September 1858
"LOCAL RECEIVING OFFICES – POST OFFICE
  Great Bolton – Moor Lane, near the Britannia
  Little Bolton – Kay Street, near the Falcon Inn
The boxes at the receiving houses in Great and Little Bolton are closed daily at six o'clock afternoon, for the London, Manchester, Birmingham, Leeds and general south mails, and the bags are taken by the letter carrier of each district to the office in Bradshawgate. After that time letters intended for the above mails may be posted at the Chief Office to half-past six o'clock, and pass without extra charge, and from that time until five minutes before the time of despatch on payment of the revenue late fee. The boxes at the local receiving houses are again closed for the second London, Liverpool, and south and north mails at nine o'clock evening, letters for the same mails may be posted afterwards at the Chief Office in Bradshawgate up to a quarter to ten o'clock without fee, and on payment in stamps of the prescribed fee up to ten minutes past ten. The fee is one stamp until ten minutes, and three stamps afterwards until five minutes before the time of despatch."

BOLTON CHRONICLE 22nd December 1855
"OPENING OF THE BOLTON NEW MARKET HALL
Bolton, within the last few years, has risen greatly in population, wealth and importance, and so rapidly have its material improvements succeeded each other, that a stranger who knew the town twenty years ago would now scarcely be able to recognise it. New churches, new institutions, public offices, and a new bank, rival each other in taste and architectural display, and the new and splendid Market Hall, whose public opening we record below, crowns the whole with classic purity and magnificence. In point of utility no building ever supplied a greater public want; while as an ornament to the town it stands unsurpassed.

The Opening Ceremony
At an early hour on Wednesday morning the sounds of the church bells pealed merrily through the air, and flags which floated from all the buildings and many of the shops in the principal streets indicated that the day was to be one of general rejoicing. The weather was all that could be desired. A number of shops were wholly and others partially closed and some of the mills and workshops ceased working early to allow such hands as were desirous of joining in the public procession, in honour of the opening, an opportunity of doing so. The various societies and bands of music intending to join in the procession began to form near the Borough Court at twelve o'clock.

The Market Hall by Gaslight
The Market Hall was crowded with people from soon after six

o'clock to ten o'clock. It was brilliantly lit up. The Gilnow Saxhorn band occupied the platform; many people had gone there in the hope of enjoying a dance, but the building was so crowded that dancing was out of the question.

The Ball

A grand ball in celebration of the opening was held in the evening at the Bath's Assembly Rooms, and was attended by the elite of the town and neighbourhood.

The first market in the hall was held on Saturday, and it being the Christmas market there was an excellent show of all descriptions of poultry.

The butchers soon disposed of their choice cuts at 7½d a pound. The show of Christmas geese was very meagre, but such as were in the market sold readily at 8d a pound.

At night the hall was so crowded that the avenues were almost impassable, and during this time several pockets were picked."

BOLTON CHRONICLE 7th May 1859
"THE DANGERS OF THE CRINOLINE
A somewhat singular, and certainly an unjustifiable interference with the "liberty of the subject", occurred on Wednesday evening last in a public thoroughfare in this town, the principal actors in which were a number of factory girls, and the sufferer the wife of a most respectable resident of the borough. It appears that this lady has a decided Continental admiration for the extremist development of that very extreme fashion, the crinoline. On the evening in question she was 'sailing' past the Market Hall when a number of factory girls, ever on the alert for fun and frolic, however mischievous or unseemly, were attracted by the really mountainous dimensions of the lady's attire, and commenced an attack upon her, the proportions of which rapidly extended until quite an uproar was created, and a considerable mob congregated. The unfortunate lady made several attempts to avail herself of cab refuge. The crinoline, however, was, it is said, too immense to enable her to squeeze through the doorways. At length, after enduring a martyrdom of insult, she obtained shelter in a druggist's shop, which was for a time besieged by her tormentors. Here she remained some hours. At length, after the subsidence of the excitement the lady was restored to her home and friends."

"*CRINOLINE – A FEW WORDS TO THE BETTER PART OF CREATION*
It is ingeniously contrived to hide all that it should show, and show all that it ought to hide. It is tight and scant where it ought to be full, and it is enormously large precisely where there is no need of factitious largeness, and it is curious to note how this particular fashion of swelled skirts arose.

Odd Items

The new Market Hall (*Bolton Almanac*)

The Empress Eugenie, being in that condition when a woman is most a woman, had need for such a form of dress and wore it. Straightaway every British maiden with a ludicrous contempt for the "eternal fitness of things" appeared in a burlesque imitation of the Empress's costume. Thus Crinoline arose, and thence has it been rising until it has reached its present enormous circumference.

It is not only that the crinoline is ugly and unmeaning – that it destroys and deforms all the beauty and sentiment of dress – that it deprives womankind by one fell stroke, of one half of its personality – that it is deceitful, graceless and impertinent.

The remedy is plain. The crinoline must be reduced, air bags collapsed, steel and gutta-percha reserved for electric telegraphs. Let women believe that they are never so adorable as when women are women and not wind bags. Let nature reserve her form, and beauty be restored to one half its province. There is no social reform so greatly needed."

BOLTON CHRONICLE 9th June 1860
"BOLTON AND MANCHESTER OMNIBUS
On and after this day (Saturday 6th June) this conveyance will leave Bradshawgate for Halshaw Moor, Clifton and Manchester daily (Sundays excepted) at 9 a.m. Returning from 31, Market Street, Manchester, at 5 p.m."

BOLTON CHRONICLE 29th December 1860
"THE WEATHER
Christmas of 1860 will be noted as one of the severest for many years. The frost all the week has been most intense. The snow which commenced its fall ten days ago still lies deep upon the ground, and the trees and hedgerows are fringed with a silvery rime, presenting a most picturesque appearance. On Christmas morning at three o'clock the mercury was at 2 degrees, or 30 degrees below freezing, and four hours later had sunk to zero."

The Borough statistics published in October 1860 emphasised the growth of Bolton in the previous ten years. The number of inhabited houses had risen 10,313 to 13,528. There had been a slight reduction in cellar dwellings from 1,579 to 1,068. Whilst the brothels in the Borough in 1850 numbered 37, the number in 1860 had risen to 70. The number of streets had risen from 474 to 620.

On the credit side the Borough now had a free library, a new workhouse, a new market hall. Conditions of labour were slowly improving, and there was a certain amount of prosperity

Odd Items

The 'deceitful and graceless' Crinoline (drawn by Anne Hargreaves)

for the artisan. The Bolton Chronicle expressed its confidence in the continuing of this prosperity, and saw no reason why the blessings of prosperity should not long continue, and prayed for the continuing peace in Europe.

The American Civil War and its consequences were not foreseen. Grim hardship and poverty were to come in the 60s with the cotton famine.

Other books by local authors published by Ross Anderson Publications and available through your local bookshop

From Affetside to Yarrow: Bolton place names and their history
W. D. Billington
The author, local historian Derek Billington, explains the origins of more than 140 place names in the Bolton area and gives many interesting historical details.
"Interesting and informative" (*Bolton Chronicle*)

Paperback   illustrated   £2.95

The Golden Age of Cookery
Tom Bridge
A lively and stimulating account of Victorian cookery, with more than 200 recipes and more than 50 photographs, by Bolton chef Tom Bridge.
"This compendium of Victorian cookery and culinary lore is fascinating and well seasoned. There are many delightful illustrations of unusual and ingenious cooking utensils" (*The Caterer*)

Hardback   illustrated   £7.95

Where Fate Leads
Harry Howarth
The moving story of a Burnley man who was a prisoner of the Japanese and worked on the notorious Burma Railway.
"The impression left with the reader is of the triumph of the will to survive" (*Lancashire Evening Telegraph*)

Paperback   £4.95

The Interview
Howard Stevens
An original and humorous first novel by a Salford man, full of surprises, earthly and otherwise.

Hardback   £7.95

For full Catalogue please write to Ross Anderson Publications Limited, Larkhill House, 160 St. Georges Road, Bolton BL1 2PJ or telephone Bolton 31289.